Vietnam Marines 1965–73

Charles Melson • Illustrated by Paul Hannon

Published in 1992 by
Osprey Publishing, Elms Court, Chapel Way, Botley,
Oxford OX2 9LP, United Kingdom.
Email: info@ospreypublishing.com
© 1992 Osprey Publishing Ltd.
Reprinted 1997, 1998, 1999, 2002, 2005

ISBN 185532 251 X

CIP Data for this publication is available from
the British Library

Series Editor: MARTIN WINDROW
Filmset in Great Britain by Tradespools Ltd., Frome,
Somerset
Printed in China through World Print Ltd.

FOR A CATALOGUE OF ALL BOOKS PUBLISHED BY
OSPREY PLEASE CONTACT:

NORTH AMERICA
Osprey Direct, 2427 Bond Street,
University Park, IL 60466, USA
E-mail: info@ospreydirectusa.com

ALL OTHER REGIONS
Osprey Direct UK, P.O. Box 140,
Wellingborough, Northants, NN8 2FA, UK
E-mail: info@ospreydirect.co.uk

www.ospreypublishing.com

Acknowledgements

Lt. Col. Nguyen Van Phan, VNMC, Retired
Maj. Edward J. Wages, USMC, Retired
Capt. Pyong Moo Rhoe, ROKMC, Retired
David A. and Katherine A. Melson,
Marine Corps Historical Center.

SOLDIERS OF THE SEA

The funeral oration by Pericles praised the Athenians for making the sea a pathway to valour. This notion can describe the peculiar mix of soldier and sailor that has earned the title of 'marine' in the modern world. Most nations that use the ocean have had, or will have, soldiers of the sea: marines.

The period following World War Two saw a number of associated Marine Corps, three of which fought together during the war in Vietnam from 1965 to 1973. These dates define this study, with the realization that fighting went on before and after. These Corps were similar formations, but each with its own history and traditions: the United States Marines, the Vietnamese Marines, and the Korean Marines. Common was a reputation for toughness on themselves and any foreign or domestic enemies; strong unit pride and loyalty; and a privileged place within the political structure of their respective countries.

They came together in the beginnings of the Cold War that witnessed a proliferation of amphibious forces in Asia — in part because of the reputation the US Marines had earned in the cross-Pacific drive against Japan and in postwar confrontations. Marine units were to be found in the Republic of China, the Republic of Korea, the Republic of Vietnam, the Philippines, Indonesia, and Thailand. These organizations were formed, with the help of foreign military aid, to fight the various conflicts to contain Communist expansion in the region. Also present at various times were other Marines from the Netherlands, France, and Great Britain.

What these Marines wore, carried, and fought with will be examined, with greatest emphasis on the US Marines, both because of the author's knowledge of the subject and because of its fundamental relationship with the other two organizations.

The 'soldier's load' was a subject examined criti-

The Commandants of the US and Korean Marines exchange gifts at a ceremony conducted in Washington, DC, in 1965, the year both organizations had combat troops in South Vietnam. On the left is Gen. Wallace M. Greene, Jr., USMC, and on the right Lt.Gen. Kong Jung Shik, ROKMC. Both wear the khaki tropical or summer service uniforms of their respective Corps. (USMC)

cally by S.L.A. Marshall and the US Marine Corps Schools early in the 1950s.[1] The Marines who went to war in 1965 should have reflected this prior knowledge. In practice, considerations of culture, supply, and circumstances were shown to have been just as important in determining what was carried into battle. Each service will be examined here to consider its insignia, uniforms, equipment, and rations. Specific designations and numbers were used to identify clothing and equipment. This was complicated by the three countries having different languages, though in most cases names were just the translation of the equivalent terms for American items. There were also different designations for the same item: a generic term used by the Marines, the supply term used to catalogue the item, and the manufacturer's jargon. The author has used here generic nomenclature with

[1] S.L.A. Marshall, *The Soldier's Load and the Mobility of a Nation* (Quantico, Va.: The Marine Corps Association, 1950).

The Commandant of the Vietnamese Marine Corps in 1965 was Brigadier-General Le Nguyen Khang, shown here as a lieutenant-general. He served as a corps commander and as a deputy on the joint general staff. He is wearing khaki shirtsleeve service uniform. (VNMC)

the vernacular terms used by Marines, trying to find a balance between regulation and reality for the decade covered, but this examination is by no means final.

The Second Indochina War

After the 1954 Geneva agreement which arranged the withdrawal of France from Indochina and the partition of Vietnam into north and south pending elections, the Americans moved to help the government of Vietnam against the Communist-supported People's Republic of Vietnam. By 1960, the date on Vietnam's campaign medal, a state of armed conflict existed between the two Vietnams and their allies.[2] This was a civil war that had international connotations for several world powers and their clients. It was a confrontation that displayed a full spectrum of violence, from individual terrorist acts and guerrilla fighting to conventional land combat, with extensive sea and air components. It was a war that continued

until the eventual defeat of the South Vietnamese by the North in 1975 and the subsequent change of regional order. It is against this background of events over almost two decades that *Vietnam Marines* should be viewed. This examination is confined to the crucial years of 1965 to 1973 during which Marines of Vietnam, Korea, and America fought the conflict together. This recognizes the fact that this was the Vietnamese people's war; nor does it fail to credit the Korean Marine contribution, that was limited by scale rather than effort.

The South-East Asia theatre of operations can be divided into North Vietnam, South Vietnam, the Tonkin Gulf littoral, and the inland frontiers of Laos and Cambodia. The country of South Vietnam consisted of administrative provinces grouped together into military regions or tactical zones numbered from I to IV, from north to south. The country was divided geographically from east to west into a coastal plain, a piedmont region, and the central highlands.

A Vietnamese Marine officer described the tactical terrain for his Korean and American allies: 'If you work in the I or II Corps area you may have the chance to climb high mountains with thick vegetation, where, in the dry season, the water problem is of more concern than the enemy. In the rainy season the water level rises considerably and currents become tremendously strong. You can send a squad patrol across a stream, and a couple of hours later this squad, on returning, will find the same stream turned into a raging river. In the III Corps you may become familiar with the Rung Sat, a wet, sticky, muddy area covered with heavy mangroves and laced with innumerable streams, many of which are not shown on your map. If you work in the IV Corps, you may be landed in U Minh Forest, an inundated terrain with thick vegetation where the water, red and dirty, rises permanently around your waist, and you will have no chance to see the sun except as a weak and indistinct light — which is what "U Minh" means.'

The enemy ranged from National Liberation Front guerrillas in South Vietnam of varying quality and quantity, to the regulars of the People's Army of Vietnam who were infiltrated into South Vietnam along the Ho Chi Minh Trail. They also defended North Vietnam with more conventional ground, air, and naval forces.[3]

[2] See Osprey's MAA 104 and 143, *Armies of the Vietnam War (1)* and *(2)*.

[3] Readers should also see Osprey's Elite 38, *The NVA and Viet Cong.*

THE VIETNAMESE MARINE CORPS

When the French departed Indochina in 1954 they left behind the fledgling armed forces of the Vietnamese Republic. Included were the riverine forces of the Navy and an assortment of Army commandos that had provided the troops for them. These had formed the river assault divisions (*Dinassaults*) that Dr. Bernard B. Fall judged as 'one of a few worthwhile contributions' to military tactics of the First Indochina War (1945–1954). The commandos were formed into two battalions and grouped at Nha Trang when the separation of Vietnam into north and south was completed. On 1 October 1954 these units were designated as the Marine Infantry of the Vietnamese Navy. In April 1956 they became known as the Vietnamese Marine Corps of the Navy, consisting of a Marine Group of two landing battalions. In 1961 the Vietnamese Marines became part of the South Vietnamese armed forces general reserve. Expansion resulted from successful employment against dissidents and bandits, which led to the formation of a 5,000-man Marine Brigade in 1962. Vietnamese Marine Corps (VNMC) influence increased, in part, due to its role in complex national politics that saw Marines involved in coups in 1960, 1963, and 1964. This continual balancing of factional power was reflected in the assignment of forces, the appointment of commanders, and the direction of the war.

The formation of their own training and replacement centres allowed the Marines to keep up to strength without relying on the Army for manpower. Both officers and men attended schools in the United States at Quantico, Virginia, where a generation of Vietnamese and Americans met and served together. One Marine commandant, Gen. Le Nguyen Khang, observed that his men were proud 'to be associated in spirit and deed with the select group of professional military men of many nations who call themselves Marines'.

Of the total of 565,350 South Vietnamese in the armed forces in 1965, just over 6,500 were Marines. This figure expanded to over 15,000 men in 1973. Total casualty figures are not available, but in the heavy fighting of 1972 alone some 1,743 Marines

Americans provided their own joint training, including this exercise on the submarine USS Perch in 1963. Vietnamese Marines watch an American sailor inflate a rubber boat on deck behind the conning tower. They wear the 'sea-wave' camouflage uniform (as they, the orginators of such camouflage, called the 'tiger-stripes') with no visible insignia except the parachute brevet worn by some on their right breast. The Marine in the centre is wearing an American style khaki web belt in contrast to the black belt worn by the others. (MAAG)

The VNMC did not have heavy weapons for much of its existence, and needed the support of the Army of the Republic of Vietnam or allied forces. These Marines ride on an ARVN M24 medium tank. They are equipped with American vintage small arms and radios. The radioman on the far right wears canvas and rubber 'jungle' boots. On his right, looking back, is a lieutenant-colonel wearing his naval style insignia on his shirt front. Uniform insignia were limited to rank devices. (VNMC)

were killed in action; another 5,302 men were wounded during the same period.

In 1965 the Vietnamese Marine Brigade was organized into a corps headquarters, two task force headquarters ('A' and 'B'), five infantry battalions, an artillery battalion, and supporting units of engineers, motor transport, military police, medical, and reconnaissance. Headquarters were located in Saigon with outlying facilities at Song Than, Thu Duc, and Vung Tau. It was commanded by a colonel, who was 'dual-hatted' as the service and the brigade commander. By this time the Vietnamese Marines were separated from the Vietnamese Navy and answerable to the high command of the Republic of Vietnam Armed Forces. Present was a 28-man advisory unit from the US Marine Corps and American field advisors were attached down to the battalion level.

By 1966 the Marines formed another battalion and realigned supporting units to become a more balanced combined-arms force. They were still lacking in armour, aircraft, and logistic support. In 1968 a Marine Division of two brigades was formed. In 1970 there were three brigades, nine infantry battalions, and three artillery battalions. Supporting units continued to be formed through the following year, reaching a peak of 939 officers and 14,290 men by the time the Americans withdrew. To face the military crisis in 1975, three additional battalions and a fourth brigade were formed in time for the South Vietnamese defeat.

Organization and Troop List

Marine Corps Headquarters
Song Than Base
Marine Training Command
Marine Division
    Headquarters Battalion
    Amphibious Support Battalion
    Signal Battalion
    Medical Battalion
    Engineer Battalion
    Antitank, Military Police, and
        Long Range Patrol Companies

Brigades 'A' and 'B', from 1968; Brigades 147, 258, 369, from 1970; Brigade 468 from 1975.

1st, 2nd, 3rd, 4th, 5th, 6th, 7th, 8th, 9th Infantry Battalions, from 1970; 14th, 16th, 18th Infantry Battalions from 1975.

1st, 2nd, 3rd Artillery Battalions

An infantry battalion had around 36 officers and 840 men arranged in four rifle companies and a headquarters and service company. Rifle companies were numbered from 1 to 4 in each battalion. A rifle company had three rifle platoons and a weapons platoon. Mortars, heavy machine guns, communications, and

A close-up of typical uniform and equipment worn by an officer in the field, a major in this case. He wears naval style black-on-green rank insignia on his helmet and collars. A name tape in unit colour and ARVN pin-on rank are worn on his right breast. He is wearing M56 individual equipment with a strobe light pouched on the right of his harness and sun glasses on the left. On his right hip is a .38 revolver, and on his left a compass carried in a first aid pouch, with 'idiot' cord holding it to his harness. This is an early camouflage uniform; note trouser pockets cut exactly like the old US OG107 fatigues. (VNMC)

medical support were grouped with the battalion headquarters. Rifle squads comprised 13 men in three fire teams of four men each.

The battalion was the primary focus of unit esprit and the paternal form of leadership that reflected the Vietnamese society. The battalions were manned by long-serving professional officers and Marines who had acquired a great deal of experience in war. Whenever possible, more than one battalion was used in conjunction with a task force or brigade headquarters to provide additional support.

Operations

As part of the national reserve, the Vietnamese Marines could find themselves anywhere from the 17th Parallel in the north to the islands of the extreme south. When assigned to a specific corps area the Marines would serve under commanders of the Army of the Republic of Vietnam. Prior to 1965 most operations were by single battalions in III and IV Corps. A variety of counterinsurgency operations were carried out, including search and destroy, search and clear, helicopter and riverine assault, and security tasks. Characteristic employment was in response to critical situations requiring rapid movement with short notice.

After 1965 the Marines deployed more to the II and I Corps areas as the war progressed away from the Delta and Capital regions. Multiple battalion operations became the norm through the use of task force headquarters. Two battalions under Task Force 'A' concluded a series of operations over a four-month

◄ *A Marine and his individual equipment are shown to good effect. He is wearing a modified, very faded camouflage uniform with a full range of insignia: a name tape and service insignia on his right breast, and on his right sleeve the 'Crazy Buffalo' of the VNMC 2nd Infantry Battalion. He is wearing the nylon and leather tropical combat boot; his pack is the popular ARVN rucksack, showing its spring steel frame. His M1 helmet and cover, M56 individual equipment, and M16 rifle are hung on a sapling. (VNMC)*

▶ *South Vietnam was the location of the main ground force effort by the US Military Advisory Command in support of the Government of the Republic of Vietnam. This map shows provinces, provincial capitals, and military regions. The war was also fought in North Vietnam, Laos, and Cambodia by units of the Seventh Air Force and Seventh Fleet. (USMC)*

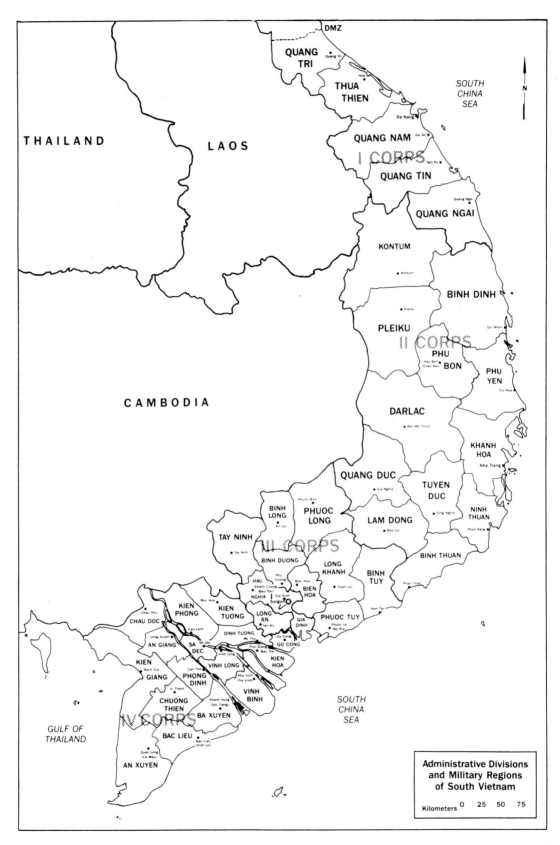

THAILAND

LAOS

DMZ

QUANG
TRI

Quang Tri

THUA
THIEN

Hue

SOUTH
CHINA
SEA

N

Da Nang

QUANG NAM

Hoi An

I CORPS

Tam Ky

QUANG TIN

Quang Ngai

QUANG NGAI

KONTUM

Kontum

BINH DINH

CAMBODIA

Pleiku

PLEIKU

II CORPS

Qui Nhon

PHU
BON

Hau Bon
(Cheo Reo)

PHU
YEN

Tuy Hoa

DARLAC

Ban Me Thuot

KHANH
HOA

Nha Trang

QUANG DUC

Gia Nghia

TUYEN
DUC

Phuoc Binh

BINH
LONG

PHUOC
LONG

An Loc

LAM DONG

Tung Nghia

Bao Loc

NINH
THUAN

Phan Rang

TAY NINH

III CORPS

Tay Ninh

BINH DUONG

LONG
KHANH

BINH
TUY

BINH THUAN

Phan Thiet

HAU
NGHIA

Phu
Cuong

Khiem Cuong
(Bao Trai)

Bien Hoa

BIEN
HOA

Xuan Loc

Moc Hoa

KIEN
PHONG

KIEN
TUONG

LONG
AN

Gia Dinh

Saigon

Tan An

GIA
DINH

PHUOC TUY

Phuoc Le
(Ba Ria)

Ham Tan

Chau Phu

CHAU DOC

Cao Lanh

DINH TUONG

My Tho

Go Cong

GO CONG

Long Xuyen

AN GIANG

SA
DEC

SA Dec

Vinh Long

Truc Giang
(Ben Tre)

KIEN
HOA

KIEN

Rach Gia

GIANG

Can Tho

PHONG
DINH

VINH LONG

Vi Thanh

Phu Vinh
(Tra Vinh)

VINH
BINH

CHUONG
THIEN

Khanh Hung
(Soc Trang)

BA XUYEN

SOUTH
CHINA
SEA

IV CORPS

GULF OF
THAILAND

BAC LIEU

Bac Lieu
(Vinh Loi)

Quan Long
(Ca Mau)

AN XUYEN

**Administrative Divisions
and Military Regions
of South Vietnam**

Kilometers 0 25 50 75

period that resulted in 444 Communists killed and another 150 taken prisoner. This included a notable engagement in April 1965 near An Thai, Binh Dinh Province, that resulted in the 2nd Infantry Battalion earning a US Presidential Unit Citation for a successful defence against an overwhelming Communist force.

From 1966 to 1968 the Marines spent more time in I Corps and conducted operations in conjunction with the Americans in this critical region. It was observed that Marines were in the field 75% of the time, then the highest figure obtained by South Vietnamese forces. During the 1968 Tet Offensive the Marines fought in both Saigon and Hue to defeat the Communist attempt at a general uprising. During this year the Vietnamese Marines maintained a casualty-to-kill ratio of one to seven.

In March 1969 the 5th Infantry Battalion earned a

Combat operations were conducted with the Vietnamese Navy's riverine forces at Ca Mau in the Mekong Delta. While these specialized boats could move units up and down rivers and canals, there came a point when the infantry still had to move on its own. These Marines leave by the bow; note M60 machine gun. They wear M1 helmets, M52 body armour, and M56 individual equipment. The Marine second from the right is armed with an M79 grenade launcher. The Marine Brigade insignia is displayed on their left shoulders. (USN)

Helicopter transport was made available by the Vietnamese Air Force and allied units. Here a VNMC squad boards a US Army UH-1D Iroquois of the 7th Air Cavalry. The stature of the Vietnamese allowed for greater numbers to be carried than with their American counterparts. They are loaded with ARVN packs, small arms, and M72 antitank rockets. (VNMC)

US Naval Unit Citation for action in III Corps, near Bien Hoa. This resulted in 73 Communists killed, 20 taken prisoner, and captured weapons. The Marines took part in the aggressive South Vietnamese external operations that coincided with the American departure: Cambodia in 1970 and Laos in 1971. The Laotian incursion was the first time a divisional command post took the field to control manoeuvre brigades.

By 1971 at least two Marine brigades remained in I Corps facing the De-Militarized Zone and the North Vietnamese. They filled, in part, the vacuum left when the Americans moved from this region. During the NVA Spring Offensive in 1972, the Vietnamese Marines were fully employed in the defence of the DMZ. At first used piecemeal under ARVN control, in June 1972 the Vietnamese Marine Division launched a counteroffensive with the Airborne Division to retake Quang Tri Province. The Marine Division established itself as a major fighting force in the month-long battle to recapture Quang Tri City. In the process they killed an estimated 17,819 North Vietnamese soldiers, took 156 prisoners, and captured more than 5,000 weapons and vehicles. At the beginning of 1973 the Marine Division was regarded by the South Vietnamese as an 'outstanding unit' of the Republic of Vietnam Armed Forces.

Insignia

Like other Marines, the Vietnamese had a series of uniforms that reflected climate and occasion: service dress with coat and tie, khaki dress, and the combat dress which became the characteristic uniform as the war went on.

The Vietnamese Marines used Navy rank insignia with Army rank titles. Eight enlisted grades existed, and seven officer grades up to sub-brigadier general (the 'one-star' grade). The rank structure reflected French influence, beginning with private, private first class, corporal, chief-corporal, sergeant, chief-sergeant, adjutant, and chief-adjutant. Officer ranks were more conventional: candidate, second lieutenant, first lieutenant, captain, major, lieutenant-colonel, and colonel. Silver braid on black backing was worn instead of the naval gold. Officers and enlisted men both wore their rank on shoulder boards. In the field this was simplified to wearing a single shoulder rank device on the front of the shirt; this resulted in a miniature version that could be fastened on a shirt or pocket button. By the end of the period, miniature rank insignia embroidered in black on green cloth were worn on the collar or headgear in the US fashion. All three types of rank badge were in use throughout the war. On occasion, Vietnamese Army pin-on rank was worn during joint operations.

Distinctive organizational emblems evolved with the service over time, and defy complete documentation. The earliest emblems included Vietnamese Navy badges worn on caps and berets in metal and embroidered forms; the emblems were gold for officers and silver for enlisted men. The distinct Marine Infantry badge had a much longer service life. It displayed crossed anchors surrounded by a plain circle, and appeared in both metal and embroidered variations. The embroidered beret badge used dark blue, and later green backing. The officer's embroidered version had a wreath of rice stalks around the crossed-anchors central design; the enlisted version had only the crossed anchors.

In 1959 a new service device was adapted with an eagle, globe, and anchor motif; this closely followed the US Marine emblem, but evolved to incorporate traditional Vietnamese features. According to an official document these included an anchor through a globe for the Marine's naval character, a five-pointed red star with Vietnam in the centre indicating combat spirit and the five parts of the world, and an eagle spreading its wings representing unyielding martial spirit. A black background stood for bravery in difficult situations — the colour of a 'death volunteer'. This design eventually formed the basis for cap, beret, unit, and service insignia. Again, there were both officer and enlisted versions. The metal cap and beret badges were gold and silver for officers and brass for enlisted. The embroidered beret badge was backed in green, and later in red.

Major variations of service and unit insignia existed. At first a full colour service emblem on a black shield was worn on the upper left sleeve, indicating the Marine Group or Brigade. Later a full colour service emblem on a green circle was worn on the right breast pocket. Finally, a full colour emblem on a green shield was worn on the upper left sleeve to indi-

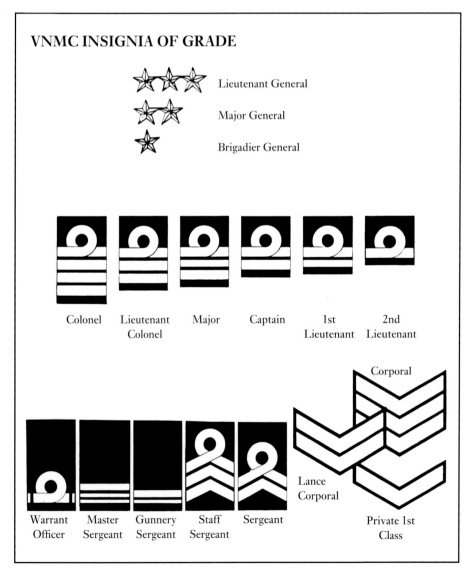

VNMC INSIGNIA OF GRADE

Lieutenant General

Major General

Brigadier General

| Colonel | Lieutenant Colonel | Major | Captain | 1st Lieutenant | 2nd Lieutenant |

Corporal

Lance Corporal

| Warrant Officer | Master Sergeant | Gunnery Sergeant | Staff Sergeant | Sergeant | | Private 1st Class |

Insignia of grade for American, Vietnamese, and Korean Marine Corps were similar, but each reflected the evolution of rank structure within their respective countries. Terms used are the equivalents of American rank rather than translations of the various national titles. See pages 18 and 28 for Korean and American insignia.

Fire support for the VNMC came from M29 81mm mortars at the battalion level, until field artillery was provided. The size and weight of the heavy weapons limited their use in rough terrain or when travelling by foot. Three types of uniform are seen in this picture: the Marine in the foreground wears the ARVN camouflage pattern, the gunner wears the VNMC pattern, while the ammunition man is wearing an olive green uniform with Marine insignia. This was the standard ARVN combat uniform and appeared to be used by the Marines as an alternative uniform. (VNMC)

cate the Marine Division, replacing the previous brigade emblem (The display of a patch on the left sleeve was in line with the ARVN practice.) Cloth emblems worn on the combat uniform were generally of a high quality woven (Bevo style) manufacture; printed variations were for general service issue.

Battalion insignia developed at the same time from coloured name tags worn over the right breast pocket. In 1966 an American advisor noted the following colours in use: 1st Battalion, blue; 2nd Battalion, purple; 3rd Battalion, olive drab; 4th Battalion, red; 5th Battalion, maroon and gold. The artillery battalion used white and red, the amphibious support battalion gold and green, and brigade headquarters were in white and green (which may have been the general service colour as well). American advisors added a tape over the left breast pocket with 'U.S. Marines' in black on green, while their name tapes on the right were in white on green. Another American advisor recalled that in 1967 he wore a brigade shoulder patch, a service emblem on his pocket, and the coloured battalion name tape.

Eventually distinct battalion patches were worn on the upper right sleeve. The infantry battalions had a series of nicknames and slogans which were reflected on their battalion insignia: 1st Bn. 'Wild Bird'; 2nd Bn. 'Crazy Buffalo'; 3rd Bn. 'Sea Wolf'; 4th Bn. 'Killer Shark'; 5th Bn. 'Black Dragon'; 6th Bn. 'Sacred Bird'; 7th Bn. 'Black Tiger'; 8th Bn. 'Sea Eagle'; and 9th Bn. 'Mighty Tiger'. The artillery units were named: 1st Bn. 'Lightning Fire'; 2nd Bn. 'Sacred Arrow'; and 3rd Bn. 'Sacred Bow'. Support and service battalions also followed this practice.

Uniforms

The field uniform was used on ceremonial occasions with the addition of white gloves, white duty belts, coloured neck scarves, white parade shoulder cords, medals, ribbons, fourragères, and white bootlaces. The Marine band had its own distinct variation on this theme that included a tailored uniform worn outside the trousers. Four classes of unit awards existed and were indicated by fourragères worn on the left shoulder, in red (gallantry), green (merit), yellow (national), and a combination of all three colours for nine previous citations.

The first combat uniform worn was the olive green shirt and trousers used by the Army and the black beret and badge of the Marine Infantry. This remained in use as basic training and fatigue clothing

Vietnamese Marines were foot-mobile infantry who moved at a traditional 2.5 miles an hour, depending on the terrain and situation. This unit is on the move in Saigon during the 1968 Tet Offensive, carrying individual and crew-served weapons. The Marine at left hefts an M18 57mm recoilless rifle; next in line is a radio operator, followed by a Marine carrying ammunition in tubes for the recoilless rifle. Of note are the M9 gas masks, M26 grenades, and M72 antitank rockets used in the house-to-house fighting. The radio operator is wearing the Marine Brigade formation insignia on his left sleeve. They are wearing the ARVN pattern camouflage uniform. (VNMC)

well after the adoption of the camouflage uniform, more from economy than sentiment. The 'sea-wave' pattern uniform, or 'tiger-stripes', was adapted in 1956 as a distinctive combat uniform. The four-colour cloth was imported and manufactured into uniforms in South Vietnam; this allowed for considerable variations in style and quality. In general it consisted of a shirt with two covered chest pockets, trousers with two thigh and two seat pockets. Pen and 'cigarette' pockets were popular modifications on the shirt sleeves and trouser legs. The Vietnamese Marines were the original users of the 'tiger-stripe' uniform, later adopted in several variations by other Vietnamese and US élite units.

By 1965, standard headgear was a green beret with Marine Infantry badge. Also worn were 'utility covers' or rain hats in 'sea-wave' camouflage pattern. The M1 helmet was used with either a net or American pattern cloth camouflage cover. A black web belt

with solid face brass buckle was issued; the US Marine open face buckle was popular as well. Footwear ranged from local 'Bata' canvas jungle boots, full leather boots, to the American tropical combat boot.

Equipment and Weapons

Individual combat equipment varied greatly over the period, from a mixture of French and American surplus to the standardized issue of M56 load-carrying equipment from the US Military Advisory Command Vietnam beginning in 1965.[1] This included the replacement of M44 and M45 combat and cargo packs with the theatre-designed semi-rigid indigenous rucksack, the 'ARVN pack'. A distinctive Vietnamese field item was the individual hammock made from parachute nylon and suspension lines.

In 1965, the Vietnamese were armed with Amer-

[1] See Osprey's MAA 205, *US Army Combat Equipments*.

ican .30 and .45 calibre small arms dating from World War Two: M1 rifles, M1 carbines, M1911 pistols, M1A1 sub-machine guns, and M1918 Browning automatic rifles. This required the use of compatible webbing and accessories to carry the ammunition and magazines for these weapons. This was followed by the issue of M16s and newer small arms by MACV at the same time as the other South Vietnamese forces. The Marines were a priority for this issue, along with the Airborne units of the national reserve.[2]

Another characteristic Vietnamese field item was the ever-present aluminium squad cooking pot, an essential item given the way the Vietnamese fed in the field. The Marines carried five days of rations of rice, dried salted fish, and canned sardines. What was not issued had to be acquired locally. A typical meal consisted of five types of food: one salted, one fried or

The face of civil war in Saigon during the Tet Offensive, 1968. In the fighting to restore order within the city, Vietnamese Marine units operated under the National Police commander Brig.-Gen. Nguyen Loan. This picture was taken moments before the well-known photographed incident when a Communist prisoner was shot through the head by Loan shortly after his capture by this mixed group of police, soldiers, and Marines. (VNMC)

roasted, vegetable soup, green vegetables, and rice. A fermented fish sauce, *nuoc-mam*, was served as a spice and source of protein. Problems also resulted if the tactical situation prevented meals from being obtained and prepared; if circumstances did not allow resupply or preparation, then the Marines would go hungry. This included any American advisors present, most of whom lost weight when serving with the Vietnamese in the field.

[2] See Osprey's Elite 29, *Vietnam Airborne.*

THE KOREAN MARINE CORPS

Formed 15 April 1949 as a company-size force, the Republic of Korea Marines have fought with the US Marines in both the Korean (1950–1953) and Vietnam (1965–1972) Wars. The ROKMC evolved from this obscure beginning to become the second largest Marine Corps in the world. By 15 January 1955 it had grown into a two-regiment division of all arms and a separate brigade based at Seoul, Chinhae, and Pohang in South Korea. Apart from combat experience, it trained with other Korean and American forces, to include air and amphibious operations. The US Marines provided advice and material support. Korean Marine Corps officers and men trained at American Marine Corps schools, and a close rapport developed over time.

The Koreans brought their own distinct culture to bear on their Marines. The Korean Marines had an image of physical toughness demonstrated on and off the battlefield, among themselves, and at times against other Korean forces. They made a virtual cult of Tae Kwon Do, a Korean martial art, to enhance their reputation for ruggedness and discipline. The Marine's declared tenets were 'Loyal to the nation; Be ever victorious; Unite as a family; Honour is worth more than life; Love your fellow countrymen'. As one veteran recalled, the reason why he volunteered for service was because the Marines had a reputation for having the hardest training and enjoyed high prestige in society. After the 1961 coup the armed forces in general dominated the South Korean social and political framework.

The Corps was organized into four main components: fleet marine forces, security forces, supporting establishment, and replacement units. In addition to security and training duties the Marines were part of the national mobile strike force, the Korean strategic reserve. The organization and equipment of these units were similar to the US Marines, 'but on a reduced scale for the equipage' according to a former commandant.

Republic of Korea forces went to Vietnam during 1965, in response to the American efforts to build a coalition to fight the Communist insurgency that had been underway since the beginning of the decade. While United Nations support failed to appear, responses came from Australia, New Zealand, the Philippines, Thailand, and Korea. Three of these countries provided combat troops, the Free World Military Assistance Forces under the control of MACV. South Korean support came in part because of their own experience with Communist aggression from North Korea.

With a total organizational strength of 27,000 men (of the 604,000 Koreans under arms in 1965), the Korean Marines considered it important to play a significant part in any combat in support of treaty obligations. As a result of this, the ROKMC contribution to the war in Vietnam ranged from 4,000 to 5,000 men at any one time from 1965 through 1972. Some 300,000 Koreans served in South Vietnam, with a peak strength of 50,000 reached in 1968. Of these,

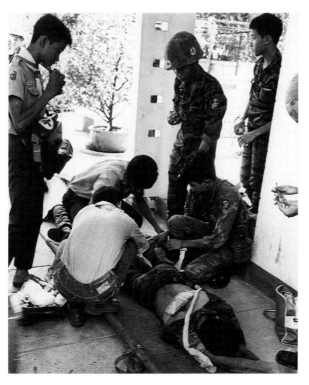

Medical treatment during fighting in Saigon in 1968. The Marine medic in the centre wears Red Cross markings on his helmet and an ARVN medical specialty insignia over his right breast pocket. The Marines depended upon personnel trained by the other armed forces for technical and specialty areas. The young man on the left is a Boy Scout. (VNMC)

4,407 Koreans were killed and almost 10,000 wounded in action.

The first Korean Marines to go to Vietnam were members of an engineer company assigned to the Republic of Korea Military Assistance Group, Task Force Dove, in March 1965. This support was soon expanded to include combat units. On 20 September 1965 the ROKMC 2nd Brigade was activated for service; this formation was called 'The Blue Dragons', after an earlier unit that had fought during the Korean War. It was established along the lines of a regimental combat team of combined arms, and manned by volunteers from the rest of the Corps. It was sent from Pusan by ship to South Vietnam, where the Blue Dragons arrived in October 1965, the first combat unit of what became the Republic of Korea Vietnam Field Force.

Organization and Troop List

ROKMC 2nd Brigade
 Brigade Headquarters
 1st Infantry Battalion
 2nd Infantry Battalion
 3rd Infantry Battalion
 5th Infantry Battalion

Supporting elements included engineers, artillery, medical, and reconnaissance units (medical personnel were from the Korean Navy). The infantry battalions each consisted of some 33 officers and 842 enlisted men organized into three numbered rifle companies, a heavy weapons company, and a headquarters and service company. Each infantry company had three rifle platoons and a weapons platoon. The basic fighting unit was the 13-man rifle squad.

Operations

The brigade was first responsible for security of the Cam Linh Peninsula in III Corps, seeing its earliest combats in the Cam Ranh and Nha Trang areas in

Beginning in 1954, American advisors started to serve with the Vietnamese Marines as part of the Marine Advisory Unit of the Naval Advisory Group. This was seldom over 50 men strong, and provided technical and tactical support to assist the VNMC. Vietnamese uniforms were worn with the addition of US Marines and name tapes over the left and right pockets and the wearing of both American and Vietnamese rank insignia. (USMC)

November 1965. In January 1966 operations began in the Tuy Hoa area of Quang Ngai Province; this involved major fighting with Communist regular forces, and over 1,500 enemy dead were recorded by the time the Koreans left. The Koreans were also responsible for the security of hamlets with a population of over 10,000. The region was a major rice-growing area, and as such was a target for subversion and terror by the insurgent forces.

American advisors served in circumstances that were different from those of USMC units in the field — particularly so in regards to food and living conditions. This advisor looks on as a meal is prepared by an orderly, known as a 'cowboy'. On the American's right shoulder is the insignia for Task Force Alpha, one of the command organizations used prior to the formation of brigades to control multiple battalion operations. (USMC)

▲ *Other advisory tasks included those associated with civic action: here Capt. John F. Stennick distributes clothing to widows of Marines killed in combat. Note the VNMC green beret and badge. He is assisted by the Vietnamese Marine social welfare officer, an ARVN Women's Armed Forces Corps captain in the ARVN camouflage uniform with VNMC insignia. (USMC)*

▶ *This Vietnamese Marine was assisted by US Marines in the replacement of his family's possessions lost when Communists attacked base housing area with rockets. The captain on the right was one of the total of 36 Women Marines assigned to Vietnam throughout the war. Her uniform is the summer service type worn by officers. (USMC)*

Like the Americans, the Koreans had to adjust in language and culture to the situation in which they found themselves. Firm security measures were tempered with civic action aimed at developing the local area, including medicine and food. Here the brigade commander proposed that it was better to make one civilian a friend than 'to make 100 VC captives'. It also earned them the local nickname of 'Devil-Catching Marines'.

In August 1966 the brigade was moved again, this time to the Hoi An area of Quang Nam Province, where it stayed for the remainder of the war. It was supported in part by helicopters, armour, and firepower from the US III Marine Amphibious Force. In February 1967 a major engagement occurred near Tra Binh with two regiments of North Vietnamese engaged by the Marines. A fourth infantry battalion was sent from Korea to reinforce the brigade in its enlarged area of operations.

Despite battlefield victories, the Korean mission in South Vietnam remained largely defensive. Joint operations were conducted, as the Americans and Koreans used the same doctrine and training; but MACV felt the Koreans lacked the heavy artillery, air assets, and supply capability for sustained combat operations. As a result, the American forces mounted large-scale operations against the North Vietnamese while the Koreans conducted cordon and search operations to clear guerrilla base areas along the coastal plain. These were successful in terms of enemy dead and captured weapons, and were based on simple, by-the-book planning, and a detailed level of effort that American and South Vietnamese forces seldom lavished on routine actions. On the pacification side — the other war — the Koreans were best at forcing the Communists out of the populated areas and providing local security. They did not have the nation-building aid that the Americans brought with them to bring the local people to the government side. This task was left to the South Vietnamese or the Americans.

By 1969 short duration small unit operations in

support of pacification were the rule, as active pursuit of North Vietnamese regulars was left to the South Vietnamese and the Americans. Even so, the Koreans continued to maintain a high ratio of enemy to friendly kills. In 1970 Korean forces averaged 150 small unit actions a day: ambushes, patrols, and general security actions. While the performance of others seemed to waver, the Koreans soldiered on.

The strategy of Vietnamization brought the withdrawal of allied combat forces from the war. This included the Koreans: the 1st and 2nd Battalions departed by December 1971, the 3rd Battalion in January 1972, and finally the 5th Battalion in February 1972. As the Marines left, there were still some 36,700 Korean soldiers in South Vietnam.

Insignia

The Koreans possessed their own versions of dress blues, winter service green, and summer service khaki uniforms. The uniforms were consciously based on those of the US Marines, with differences based on national traditions and sources of supply.

The Korean Marine insignia of grade reflected their rank structure based on the naval system, although the Korean forces used a common system of insignia by the time of the Vietnam War. There were seven enlisted grades, and seven officer grades up to the rank of colonel. The lowest rank was apprentice, followed by Marine first; second and third class (equating to the American private, private first class, and corporal). The non-commissioned officer structure started with sergeant, then staff sergeant, technical sergeant, and master sergeant. All of these were indicated by chevrons, with senior non-commissioned officers referred to as 'chief' in the naval fashion. Officer grades compared to the American warrant officer, second lieutenant, first lieutenant, and captain, using silver diamonds (gold for warrant officers) symbolizing the scales of a turtle or dragon.

ROKMC INSIGNIA OF GRADE

 Lieutenant General

Major General

Brigadier General

| Colonel | Lieutenant Colonel | Major | Captain | 1st Lieutenant | 2nd Lieutenant | Warrant Officer |

| Master Sergeant | Technical Sergeant | Staff Sergeant | Sergeant | Corporal | Private 1st Class | Private |

Assistance from allied forces arrived in strength in 1965. One of the first Republic of Korea Marine Corps units was an Engineer Company with the Republic of Korea Military Assistance Group Vietnam, Task Force Dove. This unit marches in Saigon on its arrival. They wear a Korean version of the M56 utility uniform and M41 packs and equipment and are armed with M1 rifles. (ROKMC)

Major, lieutenant-colonel, and colonel repeated a similar pattern in silver with the addition of a wreath of bamboo leaves around a diamond, symbolizing virtue. General officers used silver stars for grades of brigadier-general, major-general, and lieutenant-general. The brigade commander was a brigadier-general, with the senior officer in the Marine Corps being a lieutenant-general (briefly during this period, full general). Insignia of rank were in metal or cloth variations, worn on headgear, on collars for officers, and pinned to the left pocket for enlisted men. Shoulder insignia was used on service uniforms and some field uniforms, but a miniature rank tab in white on black appeared to be standard in South Vietnam.

The Corps' colours were scarlet and gold, and this was reflected in a woven name tape of a Marine's name and number worn over the right pocket, in yellow characters on a red background. Service loyalty was stressed over unit loyalty, and the only organizational insignia worn on the utility uniform was the stamped black ink service emblem on the left breast pocket. This was composed of a bellicose eagle, an army star, and a naval anchor to symbolize the capabilities of the Marines. The characters stood for 'Korean Marines'. Task Force Dove personnel, including Marines, wore an embroidered patch based on the red, white, and blue Korean national emblem on their left shoulder. The ROKMC 2nd Brigade had a unit emblem as a decorative device on signs, plaques, and letterhead. The closest it came to being a uniform item was on the locally manufactured 'beer can' pins informally worn after the fashion of American and South Vietnamese. Dress occasions brought forth white gloves, dark green neck scarves, gold shoulder cords, white duty belts and brass fittings, and white boot laces added to the basic field uniform.

Uniforms

Headgear consisted of a 'utility cover' in olive green or camouflage cloth with a black stamped service emblem on the crown. The M1 steel helmet was worn with a camouflage cloth cover; the pattern was either the unique Korean design or the same leaf arrangement as the American forces. Issue and field expedient bands were used to hold foliage in place.

The utility uniform was the same cap, shirt, and trousers as the US Marine's M56 and M58 utilities. Some of these came from American stocks, complete with US Marine service emblems; other uniforms were manufactured in South Korea along similar patterns. After arriving in South Vietnam, a decision was made to provide a camouflage uniform for general issue. The uniform was a variation of the camouflage uniform that was a special issue used by Korean Marine reconnaissance and raider troops. It became the standard uniform of all the South Korean forces in Vietnam and consisted of a distinctive five-colour design in a spotted pattern; with wear this faded to a

two-colour green appearance. The initial camouflage uniform had the same design as the M58 utilities, though later variations were simplified, with exposed buttons and patch pockets without flaps. White, and later olive green, underwear was similar to the American issue. An open face brass belt buckle and khaki web belt were used with the field uniform. Occasionally seen was a silver closed face version stamped with the Korean Marine emblem, normally used with the service uniform. Korean full leather combat boots were worn, even after tropical combat boots were made available from the Americans; these had a rubber sole and heel, and a black rough-out finish.

American and Korean versions of the M43 field jacket were used, in some cases with name tapes over the left pocket and rank insignia on the sleeve or shoulder straps. American issue knit sleeping shirts and rain suits were common. In general, the Koreans were well supplied and equipped. Their appearance was consistent, exhibiting a high degree of uniformity and discipline in personal appearance.

Equipment

Individual equipment showed the close association with the United States and military assistance programmes. There was a mix of items based on the M41 pattern modifications of the US Army's M10 family of individual gear. This continued in South Vietnam, as the Koreans were supported by the MACV Army-

US Marines arrived in force in South Vietnam by 1965, bringing with them technology and manpower that would change the war's tempo and intensity. In one of several small-scale amphibious landings, members of the 26th Marines land on the Batangan Peninsula in I Corps of South Vietnam. Called special landing force operations, more than 72 of these landings were made by US Marines up to 1969, with other landings being conducted with allied forces. (USMC)

based supply system, which had the Marines receiving M56 load-carrying equipment early on. This included the full range of components from the individual equipment belt, suspenders, ammunition cases, utility pouches, and combat field pack. The indigenous 'ARVN' rucksack replaced a mixture of M44 and M45 combat and cargo field packs. Armoured vests were standard American items: a mix of M52, M55, and M69 body armour.

The Koreans arrived in Vietnam armed with the American .30 and .45 calibre series of weapons of the previous decades — the M1 rifles and carbines, M1911 pistols, M1A1 Thompson sub-machine guns, M1918 Browning automatic rifles, and M1919 Browning light machine guns. This was reflected in the cartridge belts, magazine pouches, and weapons accessories used (This was not necessarily a disadvantage, as these were the same weapons used by the South Vietnamese forces). This continued until they were supplied with the M16 rifle, M60 machine gun,

and other small arms from MACV by 1967 — earlier, in fact, than their availability to US Marine units, who had a separate supply 'pipeline' and more units to equip.

Rations for the Korean Marines fell in between the needs of the Americans and the Vietnamese. The Koreans received and consumed American field rations which freed them from foraging when deployed. They were also able to modify A and B rations to their liking when in more stable base environments. This allowed for basics such as rice and delicacies like *kim-chi* (red peppers, garlic, and ginger), a preferred relish with meals.

▲ *LVT5 amphibious tractors of the 3rd Amphibian Tractor Battalion conduct joint operations with Korean Marine units south of Chu Lai during Operation 'Dragon Fire'. The ROKMC 2nd Brigade did not have the degree of support available to the* *Corps and Division structured American Marines. The weapon is a Browning .30 calibre machine gun; the man wears the standard M1 steel helmet and M55 body armour used by both Marine Corps. (USMC)*

THE UNITED STATES MARINE CORPS

The traditional date for the founding of the US Marines is 10 November 1775. In various forms, they had served in most of the official and unofficial conflicts that the United States engaged in, from 'the halls of Montezuma to the shores of Tripoli', as the song goes. The Marines provided several brigades in World War One and six divisions in World War Two. Despite popular appeal, it took a National Defense Act in 1947 to establish the current Marine Corps of three divisions, three aircraft wings, and a reserve. This confirmed the Corps' position within the defence establishment at a fixed minimum size.[1]

Even with this mandate, the Marines were hard pressed to field a division and an air wing to fight in Korea in 1950. There, an assault landing at Inchon continued the Marine Corps mission of amphibious operations. Following the recapture of Seoul the

[1] See Osprey's Elite 2, *The US Marine Corps since 1945.*

◀ *American Marines brought with them extensive logistics and service backing that allowed a build-up of forces far from the United States. This all-terrain fork lift is bringing 105mm artillery ammunition* *ashore from a landing craft. The Marines built up a base area from scratch at Chu Lai and moved into existing facilities at Da Nang. Both areas were in South Vietnam's I Corps region. (USMC)*

Sergeant John R. McDermott, a Marine combat artist, captured the subject of uniforms in combat when he observed the differences in field dress worn by American Marines and soldiers in the Pacific theatre in 1945. These sometimes subtle, or sometimes glaring variations continued through the Korean, Vietnam, and Persian Gulf conflicts. (USMC)

Marines advanced to the Chosin Reservoir, where they met the Chinese Communist army as it entered the war. After offensives, counteroffensives, seemingly endless periods of trench warfare, and occupation duty, the last Marine ground forces were withdrawn by March 1955. One lesson of the conflict was in the use of helicopters as a means of 'vertical envelopment'.

Major bases were maintained at Quantico, Virginia; Camp Lejeune, North Carolina; Camp Pendleton, California; and throughout the Pacific region. Headquarters was in Arlington, Virginia, outside Washington, DC. The Marines continued to evolve and expand through conflicts in Lebanon in 1958, Cuba in 1962, and the Dominican Republic in 1965. By then, of the 2,660,000 Americans in uniform, 193,000 were Marines. This total increased to more than 317,000 at the peak of the Vietnam War.

When the major commitment in South-East Asia began the Marine Corps was well trained, organized, and equipped for conventional operations. In Vietnam it was confronted by what one early commander there, Gen. Lewis W. Walt, described as a 'strange war, strange strategy'. Marine advisors had been present in South Vietnam since the early 1950s. The first tactical units sent were helicopter squadrons in 1962. The initial elements of the III Marine Amphibious Force arrived on 8 March 1965. An estimated 500,000 Marines served in Vietnam over the years 1962 to 1975. This amphibious force reached a maximum strength of 85,881 (of the more than 501,000 Americans serving in-country) in 1968. During the war, 14,809 Marines were killed, died, or were posted missing; another 88,635 were wounded.

Organization and Troop List

III Marine Amphibious Force
Force Headquarters
1st Marine Division
   Headquarters Battalion
   1st, 5th, 7th Marine Regiments (infantry)
   11th Marine Regiment (artillery)
   1st Reconnaissance Battalion
   1st Force Reconnaissance Company
   1st Tank Battalion
   1st Amphibian Tractor Battalion
   1st Antitank Battalion
   1st Engineer Battalion

Marine drivers are lined up for an inspection during 'motor stables' with their M151 quarter-ton utility truck, the Vietnam era 'jeep'. Illustrated is the standard field uniform worn on arriving in South Vietnam in 1965: the olive green cotton sateen utility uniform and cover, white underwear, khaki web belt, and black leather field boots. This remained the standard Marine Corps field uniform throughout the war; other uniforms were considered special issue items limited to the war zone. (USMC)

1st Motor Transport Battalion
7th Motor Transport Battalion
11th Motor Transport Battalion
1st Medical Battalion
1st Shore Party Battalion
3rd Marine Division
  Headquarters Battalion
  3rd, 4th, 9th Marine Regiments (infantry)
  12th Marine Regiment (artillery)
  3rd Reconnaissance Battalion
  3rd Force Reconnaissance Company
  3rd Tank Battalion
  3rd Amphibian Tractor Battalion
  3rd Antitank Battalion
  3rd Engineer Battalion
  11th Engineer Battalion
  3rd Motor Transport Battalion

  9th Motor Transport Battalion
  3rd Medical Battalion
  3rd Shore Party Battalion
  26th, 27th Marine Regiments (infantry)
1st Marine Aircraft Wing
  Marine Wing Headquarters Squadron
  Marine Aircraft Group 11 (fixed-wing — attack)
  Marine Aircraft Group 12 (fixed-wing — attack)
  Marine Aircraft Group 13 (fixed-wing — fighter)
  Marine Aircraft Group 15 (fixed-wing — fighter)
  Marine Aircraft Group 16 (helicopter — utility)
  Marine Aircraft Group 36 (helicopter — utility)
  Marine Wing Support Group 17
  Marine Air Control Group 18
Provisional Marine Aircraft Group 39 (helicopter)
Force Logistics Command
  Headquarters
  Maintenance Battalion
  Supply Battalion
  1st Military Police Battalion
  1st Radio Battalion
  5th Communications Battalion
  7th Engineer Battalion
  9th Engineer Battalion
3rd, 9th Marine Amphibious Brigades
Special Landing Force — Seventh Fleet, to 1970; thereafter 31st, 33rd Marine Amphibious Units (fleet landing force when afloat)

The units sent to Vietnam illustrated the combined arms nature of the US Marine Corps that made it a fourth branch of the American armed forces. The III Marine Amphibious Force was a combat organization that could be considered a miniature army and air force. Under a single commanding general were all of the elements for sustained combat in the air and on the ground, with logistical backup.

Each infantry regiment had three 1,193-man battalions numbered 1 to 3. Each had four 216-man rifle companies, which were lettered 'A' to 'D' in the 1st Battalion, 'E' to 'H' in the 2nd Bn., and 'I' to 'M' in the 3rd Bn. ('J' was not used as a designation). At the battalion headquarters were mortars and recoilless rifles. In practice battalions, and even companies, were used in mixed task forces. The basic 14-man rifle squad included a squad leader, grenadier, and three fire teams of four men each.

Operations

Elements of the 3rd Marine Division and the 1st Marine Aircraft Wing were initially sent to Da Nang, in I Corps, to secure the air base located there. At this time III Marine Amphibious Force's area of operations covered 249 square miles, including the coastal enclaves of Phu Bai, Da Nang, and Chu Lai. The American Marines had four tasks to accomplish: to defend the critical airfields, destroy Communist combat forces, destroy Communist subversive infrastructure, and conduct civic action to support the government of South Vietnam.

In June 1965 the Marines moved out of the coastal areas to seek the enemy. In August, Operation 'Starlight' was the first large-scale American attack against Communist main force units. Marine air and ground elements followed with several other operations as the war enlarged. Units arrived from the 1st Marine Division to provide additional forces. By the end of the year the Marines had conducted 50 regimental or battalion size employments, 390 company size actions, and had carried out more than 21,000 patrols and ambushes.

The year 1966 saw continued expansion of the effort in Vietnam with the arrival of the remainder of the 1st Marine Division. Operation 'Hastings' in July marked the beginning of many hard-fought battles with the People's Army of Vietnam along the DMZ. In October the 3rd Marine Division moved its headquarters to Phu Bai and the 1st Marine Division left Chu Lai for Da Nang as the war picked up in the northern provinces. As the Marine emphasis shifted north, MACV moved US Army units in to occupy the vacated areas in the south of I Corps. By May 1967 the area under Marine influence had expanded to 1,700 square miles, encompassing 183 villages, and increased the number of civilians affected by its presence to more than a million.

During the first two years in combat, Marines accounted for more than 22,500 Communist troops killed in action; another 2,100 were captured, along with 3,500 weapons. Marine units completed more than 140 major operations and 267,000 small unit actions. Civic action programmes resulted in the building of 97 bridges, 61 wells, and more than 2,100 miles of road. Medical treatment was provided to more than 1,780,000 South Vietnamese. In June 1967 the Marines in-country numbered approximately 76,000 men, and the III MAF commander, Lt.Gen. Robert

The Marines brought their own air force in the form of the 1st Marine Aircraft Wing. It fielded fixed and rotary wing combat and support aircraft to support Marine ground units and other American forces. Ordnance men load 500 pound general purpose bombs on an A-4 Skyhawk from Marine Aircraft Group 12. They wear the informal working dress of the rear areas. The centre man has a K-Bar fighting knife on his belt, the man on the left wears ear protection against the engine noise. (USMC)

This Marine Aircraft Group 16 flight of CH-46 Sea Knight transport helicopters are lined up at a forward airfield prior to a combat operation. Browning .50 calibre heavy machine guns protrude from port and starboard windows. The flight-suited individual in the centre is inspecting rotor blades, while ground troops are being briefed in the background. (USMC)

E. Cushman Jr., had operational control of almost 123,000 Free World Forces in I Corps.

Communist pressure along the DMZ increased as 1968 began. The enemy concentrated on Khe Sanh, and then launched an abortive general uprising throughout South Vietnam. Marines were crucial in the subsequent battles for Hue and Dong Ha. Additional forces were airlifted from the United States on short notice, and III MAF expanded to what the MACV commander, Gen. William C. Westmoreland, called 'the largest field Marine command that our country has ever deployed'. At the time it controlled units from all the American services, South Vietnamese, and Korean forces. The largest Marine helicopter assault, Operation 'Meade River', smashed enemy base camps and sanctuaries as the year ended.

In 1969 US Marines numbered 81,000 in I Corps. As III MAF completed its fifth year in Vietnam, it looked back on a year of unparalleled success in which the largest Communist ammunition and supply dumps of the war had been uncovered in Operation 'Dewey Canyon'. The 3rd Marine Division left for Okinawa in November 1969. This began the departure of Marines from Vietnam, and by the end of the year only 55,300 remained in-country.

In March 1970 the US Army took control of the American effort in I Corps. The Marines continued to carry the war to the enemy, but large-scale operations diminished in number as redeployment continued. The Vietnamese armed forces shouldered an increasing share of the fighting as the Americans left. By December 1970 some 25,000 Marines remained. In almost six years of combat, Marines had participated in approximately 400 major operations and innumerable small unit actions. The Marine combat

An aircrew briefing showing the flight uniform and equipment used by helicopter crews in the late war years. The olive green flying suit was made of Nomex fire retardant material. The black leather flying boots had a steel safety toe. The pilot on the left is wearing a combination life preserver and survival vest. Fixed wing crews wore additional equipment. (USMC)

effort lived up to previous Corps performance.

The 1st Marine Division fought in more than 160 named operations, including 'Hastings', 'DeSoto', and 'Go Noi Island'. During the Tet Offensive it was the first US unit called to support the drive to recapture Hue. Civic action programmes in the hamlets were part of the division's mission throughout the period, and provided much-needed medical assistance as well as the rebuilding of schools, hospitals, roads, and market places.

The 3rd Marine Division had been the vanguard of the US ground forces and participated in virtually every phase of the war until it left; in all, this included over 120 named operations. This was the division that withstood the onslaught of four enemy divisions at Khe Sanh. The division first developed the tactic of mutually supporting fire bases to cover infantry advances. In its pacification work, it pioneered the use of the 'county fair' approach for securing the loyalty of rural Vietnamese.

The 1st Marine Aircraft Wing was fully deployed in Vietnam to give close support to ground forces and hinder enemy movements. Its helicopters and fixed-wing aircraft provided the lift and fire support to operate at extreme distances from fixed bases. The Marine air and ground concept was applied on an unprecedented scale starting during Operations 'Meade River' and 'Dewey Canyon'. Marine air also took part in the tactical bombing of North Vietnam.

The last of III MAF's major combat elements left Vietnam by June 1971. There remained some air and ground units until the final ceasefire in January 1973. After that, the only remaining Marines were those with the American Embassy's security guard.

Insignia

Marine rank insignia were of the metal pin-on type, in black for enlisted men and bright silver or gold for officers. They were worn on both collars, if worn at all in the field. Enlisted rank was worn at an angle to the front edge of the collar and officer rank was worn centred and parallel to the front collar edge. During the Vietnam War the Marines had 12 enlisted grades and 14 grades of warrant and commissioned officers. Various gold and silver metal qualification badges ('wings'), mainly for aviation skills, were worn at individual option over the left shirt pocket. Medal ribbons were only worn on service uniforms.

The US Marines emphasized service rather than unit loyalty. To enhance this, insignia was not worn other than the Corps emblem found on the cap and combat uniform. This was the traditional eagle, globe, and anchor insignia stencilled on the left breast

USMC helicopter support was also provided to other American and allied forces; these two CH-46s from Marine Aircraft Group 36 lift off after a resupply run to ROKMC 2nd Bde. units north of Hoi An. The Koreans unload cases of field rations inside a defensive perimeter of their characteristically well-constructed field fortifications. They wear both olive green and camouflaged clothing. (USMC)

pocket over the heart. The utility cap was marked thus by the manufacturer. By the time of the Vietnam War, all shirts were issued unmarked and the individual used heat transfer or stencils to apply insignia to the shirt. With unit replacement of clothing in Vietnam, these 'USMC transfers' were not always available, or used by exception at whim. The field jacket,

as unit property, was seldom marked like this. Unit insignia were approved for aviation squadrons for use on flight clothing. The divisions and wing had symbols that were based on the shoulder patches used during the Second World War. These were to be found on equipment, signs, plaques, and informal items.

Uniforms

The issue M1 steel helmet with single chin strap was the same as worn in World War Two and the Korean War. A reversible camouflage cloth helmet cover was worn — one side had a green leaf pattern, and the other a spotted brown design that soon faded with use far beyond that found in Army units. Use of World War Two or Korean War covers in 'duck hunter' camouflage was not uncommon. Bands were worn to hold foliage in place on the helmets; sometimes these were made of rubber inner tube material, or were Army issue olive green elastic bands. The cloth cap ('utility cover') was worn, often with rank insignia fixed to the crown. It had a black printed eagle, globe, and anchor on the front. The cap was olive green — what Marines called 'sage green' — throughout the war; the more faded the green, the better! When not in use, it was folded and kept in the helmet liner. In rear areas it was starched to provide shape. Bush hats of all types were available (olive green, ERDL[1] camouflage, or 'tiger-stripe'); most were not official except in ground reconnaissance units, and were purchased or traded from the local economy. Sweat rags improvised from olive green towels or cravat bandages were worn around the neck or head. A sweat band could also be made from the strap and safety pin of the issued cloth ammunition bandoleer.

Identification tags ('dog tags') were oblong aluminium tags with an individual's name, service number or social security number, religion and blood type; issued in pairs, they were worn around the neck on a chain or attached to the boot laces.

Three shirt and trouser uniform combinations were used during the war. They were, in chronological sequence: in use from 1962, Utilities, Man's Cotton Sateen OG107; from 1966, Jungle Utilities, Man's Cotton Wind Resistant Rip Stop Poplin OG107; and from 1968, Camouflage Utilities, Man's Camouflage Cotton Wind Resistant Rip Stop Poplin.

[1] Engineer Research Development Laboratory

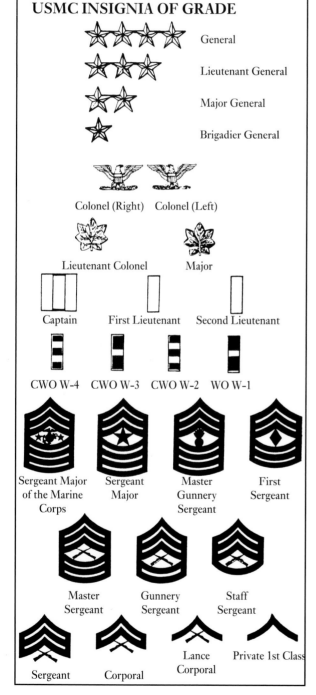

USMC INSIGNIA OF GRADE

General

Lieutenant General

Major General

Brigadier General

Colonel (Right)   Colonel (Left)

Lieutenant Colonel   Major

Captain   First Lieutenant   Second Lieutenant

CWO W-4   CWO W-3   CWO W-2   WO W-1

Sergeant Major of the Marine Corps   Sergeant Major   Master Gunnery Sergeant   First Sergeant

Master Sergeant   Gunnery Sergeant   Staff Sergeant

Sergeant   Corporal   Lance Corporal   Private 1st Class

▲ *This ROK Marine captain, a company commander, was providing security with his unit to US Marine land-clearing operations on the coastal region near Hoi An.*

He wears the Korean camouflage uniform over an American sleeping shirt. It clearly shows the placement of rank, service, and name insignia. (Wages)

▲ *An infantry leader with the 9th Marines displays a variety of personal equipment in the field during the middle of the war. He has an M1 helmet with camouflage cover, M55 body armour, M45 suspenders, pistol belt with K-Bar knife, M42 steel snap link, M42 first aid pouches for compass and field dressing, .45 pistol magazine pouch, and (just visible on his right hip) black leather holster for the M1911 pistol. His uniform is the ERDL camouflage utilities. He holds a Communist RKG3 antitank grenade in his right hand. (USMC)*

The jungle and ERDL-pattern camouflage utilities were designed for use in Vietnam and were of a light, strong, quick-drying cloth. The jacket had four pockets and was worn outside the trousers. The trousers had four pockets on the hips and two on the trouser legs. Olive green and camouflaged utilities were worn as issued in theatre, though issue was generally later than to Army units. The wearing of different kinds was sometimes concurrent because of supply system quirks. As the war progressed and Army items were relied upon, Marine units began to look more and more like their soldier counterparts; but the camouflage uniform was a distinct issue to Marines as a whole.

Shirt sleeves were worn rolled up or down. For a time, sleeves were allowed to be cut off, and were left frayed or hemmed. The sateen utilities worn by the first Marine units to arrive in Vietnam might have embroidered name tags over the left breast pocket for those deploying from Okinawa (then an American administered part of Japan). In the field, the OG sateen shirt was worn outside the trouser waist to circulate air. White underwear was used until locally dyed or manufactured olive green items were available; often no underwear was worn for comfort in the humid environment. Sometimes seen were Special Service (this was a welfare and recreation agency)-funded olive green undershirts and sweat shirts with wing or division names printed over 'Vietnam' on the front in black block letters.

Trousers were worn bloused around the boot top with 'blousing garters' rather than being tucked into the boot top in the Army style. The issue khaki web belt with an open face brass buckle was used, supplemented by 'jungle' belts made from suspender straps, or even captured North Vietnamese army belts. The web belt remained popular as it was one of the few Marine Corps-unique items worn, even though subdued colours were more practical. It also doubled as a cargo strap to secure ammunition boxes, sleeping bags, etc. Socks were worn, with a spare pair kept in a plastic radio-battery bag to rotate when one pair was wet. They were also used to carry ration cans tied to the back or side of the pack, and to pad or silence other items of equipment. At first leather combat boots were worn, including a Marine Corps-unique rough-out version with hook and eye closures. The Marines had gone to all black leather in 1963, so that by 1965 most leather gear was issued black or polished black, including boots. Green nylon and

black leather tropical combat boots (jungle boots) were preferred, and worn as available, again later than in Army units.

The M43 and M65 field jackets were available during cold weather, in some cases from unit stocks or issued to individual replacements on Okinawa. An infantry commander at Khe Sanh recalled that field jackets and wool shirts were issued to his unit during the 'winter' monsoon period of November 1967 to February 1968. This shirt was a Marine Corps uniform item of cold weather clothing that served the same purpose as the Army polyester knitted sleeping shirt. The theory was that these could be kept dry in the pack during the day, then used at night in place of a wet utility shirt. In practice they were worn under the shirt in cold or wet weather. There are some photographs of it serving as an outer garment.

Rain suits were issued to armour and motor transport crews. The government issue parka and coverall were made of olive green rubberized fabric that darkened in colour when wet. Korean, Okinawan, or Vietnamese-made local items were lighter in weight and could be in any colour, though usually green or camouflage. Velcro closures were added during the war to the rain suits and field jackets without a change to the model designation. Rain suits were worn in lieu of the more restrictive poncho in rear areas and in the field. Everyone had a poncho that could be used as a

The evolution of personal equipment by the middle of the war is seen on this well-organized rifleman from the 26th Marines as he searches a bunker. His camouflage pattern utilities are loose over jungle boots for ventilation. He wears M55 body armour over an olive green undershirt, topped by a bandoleer of M16 magazines. His pack is the ARVN rucksack with shirt, poncho, and rations. On top is an M17 field protective mask and carrier, with the handle of a K-Bar knife showing over the canteen on his left hip. (USMC)

rain garment, shelter, ground sheet, or body bag. A spun nylon poncho liner was issued; this served as a lightweight blanket and insulated the poncho when sleeping in the open.

The M55 protective body armour — the 'flak jacket', with its fabric-covered 'rope ridge' on the shoulder, and angular plates — was characteristic, although Army M52 and M69 versions were also used. All were worn over an undershirt or bare skin in hot weather. Eyelets on the waist of the jacket allowed some items of equipment to be hooked directly to it so that cartridge belt and harness could be dispensed with. Later models had two pockets added to the lower front. They were designed, like the helmet, to protect from fragmentation and were not bulletproof. Body armour was best suited for static positions and gun crews, but became a permanent part of the equipment issue for a number of reasons. Separate armoured 'shorts' existed, but were seldom used, except to sit on by vehicle and aircraft crews.

Equipment

Individual combat equipment was called '782 gear' by Marines. This was the Marine Corps M41 system used in World War Two and the Korean War; in fact, items with 1941 date stamps were still being issued. The later M61 cartridge belt had snaps along its

Regulations did not ensure uniformity, as shown by this photograph of Marine general officers in Da Nang in 1969. Jungle, camouflage, and sateen pattern uniforms are all being worn with a variety of accessories. From the left are 1st Marine Division commander Maj. Gen. Ormond Simpson; III Marine Amphibious Force deputy commander Maj. Gen. George Bowman; III Marine Amphibious Force commander Lt.Gen. Herman Nickerson; Commandant of the Marine Corps Gen. Leonard F. Chapman; Vietnamese I Corps commander Lt.Gen. Hoang Xuan Lam; 1st Marine Aircraft Wing commander Maj.Gen. William Thrash; and III Marine Amphibious Force chief of staff Brig.Gen. George Dooley. (USMC)

length to hold the M61 magazine pouch for the M14 rifle. The pistol belt had only one such snap for the left side. This difference became irrelevant as the Army M56 individual equipment belt became standard. This equipment was of heavy cotton canvas and blackened metal construction. Nylon edging began to appear after 1967, but it was not on the original issue. Complete nylon and plastic construction were seldom seen. Like velcro, nylon material was a modification that did not affect model numbers.

A fighting load consisted of a web belt; an individual field dressing and M42 first aid case or a jungle first aid kit (the M56 utility pouch held the standard field dressing but also carried cigarettes, compass, whistles, etc.); two to four M61 magazine pouches for

the 20-round M14 rifle magazine (or two or more M56 universal pouches each with three 20-round M16 rifle magazines); and two or more canteens with cases, worn on the belt or pack. A rifle bayonet (M6 for the M14 and M7 for the M16), or K-Bar combat knife, and an M16 bipod carrying case and cleaning kit, could also be worn on the belt. This 'war belt' was suspended from a pair of M41 belt suspender straps. The Army's M56 suspenders ('H' harness) were superior, and preferred when obtainable.

The fighting knife was issued to everyone who carried a pistol, including machine gunners, grenadiers, corpsmen, officers, and staff non-commissioned officers. The 'K-Bar' was in fact made by Camillus rather than the original KaBar company. It was not marked USMC, and came in a very dark brown leather sheath. It or other knives were also carried at personal whim. Most wore knives on their pistol belt on the left side. The affectation of wearing a sheath knife inverted on the load-bearing harness was inconvenient, and sometimes dangerous if drawn across the throat or chest. In ground reconnaissance units there was a habit of carrying the knife on another belt made from a cut down suspender strap so that it was never separated from the Marine. The utility of the 'fighting' knife was more as a general pur-

pose tool, serving everything from a hammer to a pry bar.

The subsistence load included anything not needed to fight and survive. It was carried in the issue pack, the M41 haversack worn as a light marching pack. This World War Two era construction of canvas, webbing, and brass fittings was almost indestructible. If correctly assembled, the straps could be tightened or loosened while on an individual's back. The marching pack, field marching pack, transport pack, and field transport pack of *Landing Party Manual* and Marine Corps Recruit Depot ('Boot Camp') fame were seldom seen or used in Vietnam. Indigenous rucksacks and US Army Special Forces rucksacks were popular and used when available or issued. Captured Chinese-made packs were also pressed into service, and were preferred to the M41 haversack because of their external pockets.

The haversack would hold the minimum possible load that a Marine could live with. The load could consist of as little as a single carry-all such as the M56 combat field pack ('ass pack'), the case from an M17A1 field protective mask, a demolitions bag or a Claymore mine bag. This was a matter of experience, with new men enduring the maximum load and the veteran shedding as much weight as possible. Gener-

1: USMC general officer, 1969
2: ROKMC general officer, 1965
3: VNMC general officer, 1970

A

1: VNMC infantry combat uniform, 1965
2: VNMC service insignia
3: VNMC officer, combat uniform, 1965

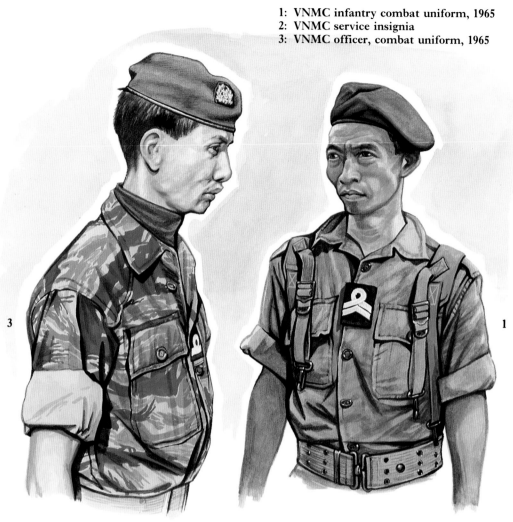

3

1

2

B

1: VNMC service dress, 1965
2: VNMC squad leader: Delta region, 1967
3: VNMC artillery officer, Saigon, 1968

C

1: VNMC parade dress, 1969
2: VNMC grenadier; Quang Tri City, 1972
3: VNMC advisor; Hue City, 1973

D

1: **ROKMC enlisted utility uniform, 1965**
2: **ROKMC service insignia**
3: **ROKMC rifleman; Tuy Hoa, 1966**

1: ROKMC infantry officer; Tra Binh, 1967
2: ROKMC insignia placement
3: ROKMC rifleman; Hoi An, 1970

F

USMC

1: USMC rifleman; Chu Lai, 1965
2: USMC service insignia
3: USMC helicopter pilot; Da Nang, 1965

G

1: USMC radio operator; Da Nang, 1966
2: USMC combat engineer; Phu Bai, 1966
3: USMC ANGLICO team B member;
   Marble Mountain, 1967

H

1: USMC mortarman; De-Militarized Zone, 1967
2: USMC armoured crewman; Hue City, 1968
3: USMC artillery officer; Khe Sanh, 1968

I

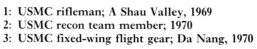

1: USMC rifleman; A Shau Valley, 1969
2: USMC recon team member; 1970
3: USMC fixed-wing flight gear; Da Nang, 1970

J

1: USMC advisor; MACV-SOG, 1971
2: USMC helicopter flight gear; Tonkin Gulf, 1972
3: USMC Embassy Guard; Saigon, 1973

K

1: Vietnamese Marine Division insignia
2: ROKMC 2nd Brigade insignia
3: US Marine Division and Wing insignia

3

1

2

ally this included a poncho, rations (sometimes stacked in a boot sock and hung off the pack or 'H' harness), toiletries, and entrenching tool ('E' tool). The M17A1 field protective (gas) mask and case were carried for use with CS and CN riot control agents (tear gas), most noticeably during the battle of Hue. Additional items depended upon terrain and weather, including poncho liners, rain suits, field jackets, sleeping shirts, spare socks, and the 'rubber bitch' air mattress. Personal touches were seen in bush hats, tiger shorts, sun glasses, extra knives and pistols.

The 'basic allowance' of ammunition carried could include 100 rounds of 7.62mm M14 ammunition in five magazines and 60-round bandoleers, or 140 rounds of 5.56mm M16 ammunition in seven magazines and 140-round bandoleers. Taping rifle magazines end to end for rapid reloading might look 'salty', but would pull the top magazine out of alignment with the bolt and cause a failure to feed; the M16 magazine catch was not adjusted to hold the extra weight; and the lower magazine picked up dirt and debris, particularly while being used in the prone position. The M79 grenade launcher was issued one per rifle squad, and allowed the infantry to knock out direct fire weapons without exposing themselves to throw hand grenades or fire rifles at an enemy position. It was a very useful weapon, but slow to reload. Rounds were carried in Claymore and demolition bags or in special bandoleers and vests.

Hand grenades carried could include two to four M26 or M69 fragmentation, M18 smoke, and M15 white phosphorus. Grenades could be a problem if left hanging off the webbing, including the purpose-designed M56 magazine pouches; the spoons would bend and break after a time, allowing the grenade to drop off, scoring your own goal. But if carried in fibreboard storage tubes or grenade pouches they could be hard to get at in a fire-fight. American M26 grenades were in demand by the Communists because they were effective and useful as booby traps: discharged and discarded M72 (LAW or LAAW) rocket tubes were filled with armed M26 grenades and fastened over a trail or other constricted area. When the covers were rigged to a trip wire, the load of grenades was dumped all at once.

Crew-served weapons (machine gun, mortar, rocket, recoilless rifle) ammunition was passed out to individual riflemen to spread the load. This might include one to three 3.5in. rocket or M72 antitank rocket rounds; one or two 81mm mortar rounds; one to three 60mm mortar rounds; illumination flares ('pop-ups'); and machine gun ammunition in boxes or belts. The M60 ammunition was carried in a waxed cardboard box inside a cloth bandoleer; these came two to a metal ammunition box, each carrying 100 rounds. The decision to carry the ammunition in the box, bandoleer, or slung across the chest depended upon the local situation and unit control. Slung ammunition was easier to carry but subject to wastage or dirt and damage. Spare barrel bags, batteries, and PRC10 or PRC25 radios might complete the load.

The term 'grunt' had the same basis in fact as the Roman legionary's nickname of 'Marius's mule'. Despite the desired body-to-load weight ratio of three to one, the typical Marine carried in excess of the postulated 50lb maximum; excessive averages

Base areas required security from attacks by rockets, mortars, sappers, and local guerrillas. These Korean Marines man a Browning .50 cal. in position to fire across a rice field near Hoi An. The gunner has an M26 grenade by his right elbow. Both wear the plain olive green utility uniform with camouflaged helmet cover. Shelter halves are used to line the fighting hole. (ROKMC)

Selected US Clothing and Equipment Weights (in pounds)

Helmet	3.5	Cleaning kit, M16	1	Magazines & 7 rds — 3	1.5
Utilities	2.26	Gas mask & carrier	2.5	M60 machine gun	23.25
Boots	2.1	Body armour	6.7	M60 tripod	11.75
Suspenders	.65	Haversack	3	M60 spare barrel bag	20.83
Belt	.84	Rations, MCI — 9 meals	18.75	M60 ammunition, 100 rds	6.5
Canteen & case, full	3.6	Poncho & liner	1.7	M79 grenade launcher	5.9
Ammunition pouch	.86	Air mattress	3	Ammunition, 40mm — 20 rds	10
Bayonet/knife	1	Field jacket	4	Claymore AP mine	5
First aid pouch	.1	Entrenching tool	4.8	M72 LAW/LAAW	5.5
Compass	.43	M16 rifle	7.25	M26 hand grenade	1.5
Flashlight	.82	Magazines & 20 rds — 7	7	M18 smoke grenade	1.25
Camouflage stick	.08	.45 pistol	2.5	PRC25 radio	26

were more like 80 to 100 pounds. This was brought about by the belief that if you did not carry something, then you did not have it. This was encouraged by the limitations of helicopter and vehicle transport once a unit was deployed on foot in the field.

The enclave strategy required a series of search-and-clear operations conducted in the populated areas of the coastal plain. Members of the 5th Marines are engaged in a local security patrol near An Hoa. Of interest is the use of the RR9/PRT4 helmet radio by members of the unit. The man on the right carries a 12 gauge shotgun and a pistol in a nonstandard shoulder holster. (USMC)

Officers and non-commissioned officers carried the same clothing and equipment as enlisted Marines. Additions would be in the form of a pistol belt consisting of an M61 belt, an M1911 .45 calibre automatic pistol and leather holster, a pistol magazine pouch holding a pair of seven-round magazines, canteens, first aid kit, and H-harness or belt suspender straps. A compass was carried in either a pouch or pocket, often tied to the belt with an 'idiot cord' made from a bootlace or parachute suspension line. A watch might be worn with the wrist strap through a button hole of the shirt or breast pocket.

Small unit leaders and commanders would have

an assortment of maps, notebooks, radio code sheets, and tactical book-keeping material needed to accomplish their tasks. As combat became more direct, frontline leaders adapted the uniform and look of the rifleman to avoid standing out. This was hard to do when followed by one or more radio operators and the headquarters element of even the smallest sized unit.

Armoured vehicle crews, like most motorized or mechanized personnel, were distinguished by the lack of gear carried by the average 'grunt'. At most they might wear body armour, pistol belt or shoulder holster, and carry an M3 sub-machine gun ('grease gun'), which was an issue item to tank, Ontos self-propelled 106mm rifle, and amphibian tractor crews. The shoulder holster was black leather and could be worn with single-strap configuration across the chest or around the waist, though it was designed to be worn with two straps, one around the chest and the other over the shoulder.

Support and service personnel were issued the same uniforms and equipment but usually in lesser amounts, and there was a tendency for the older models to remain in use with these units. Aviation personnel — pilots, naval flight officers, and aircrewmen — were provided flight equipment in addition to uniform items. This came through naval air supply channels and included: protective helmets, sun glasses, flying suits, jackets, gloves, and flying boots. Differences existed based on the type of aircraft flown, either helicopters or fixed wing. Some individual combat equipment was used, including body armour and web gear, according to individual circumstances.

Uniform and Equipment Practice

Though American combat uniforms in Vietnam appeared the same, the alert or knowledgeable observer can detect differences between soldiers and Marines. This was due to unique procurement and supply practices, and the local terrain and situation. Factors included individual or unit preference, authorized weapons, unit missions, and the type of organization (combat, support, or service). The supply system and personal choice was not sufficiently universal to allow completely uniform appearance. Marines also had an affection for 'salty' clothing and equipment — they preferred older items, to convey an image of experience.

Continuous contact with the local population emphasized the need for a 'hearts and minds' approach to mitigate the effects of war among the civilian population. Navy Hospitalman Donald W. Vogt with the 1st Marines treats a villager near Da Nang. He wears an M1 helmet and camouflage cover, M55 body armour over an undershirt, web belt, camouflage trousers, and jungle boots. His pistol belt holds two M10 canteens and covers, and holster. By his knee is a 'Unit One' bag with basic medical supplies. (USMC)

Marines were assigned a 13-month Vietnam tour, and few were in a position (or cared) to bring clothing with them or to return clothing and equipment to the United States afterwards. When ordered overseas, most were limited to a khaki summer uniform and an 'overnight' or 'AWOL' (for 'absent without leave') bag of about 25 pounds. Exceptions were those who deployed as units by ship or aircraft, who already had field uniforms and equipment. Departure by commercial airlines was from Travis and Norton Air Force Bases in California via Okinawa. On Okinawa, personnel were processed through Camp Hague and then on to Vietnam, where they were issued clothing and equipment at the unit level. The unit replaced these items as required throughout the stay in Vietnam, sometimes by the reissue of salvaged clothing and equipment. Marines left a duffel bag ('sea bag'), or footlocker for officers and staff non-commissioned officers, in the rear at a unit's base camp, with spare uniforms and belongings. In some cases these might not be seen again until the Marine rotated back to the United States.

◄ For ground units, routine hardships were the terrain and the weather. Infantrymen from 3rd Marines manage to light cigarettes in a downpour just below Mutters Ridge near the DMZ. The Marine on the right wears rain suit trousers, while the man on the left has on the parka from a rain suit. Made of rubberized fabric, they were hot and wet, if waterproof. They were worn in preference to the poncho, which was noisy and restricted movement and weapons-handling. (USMC)

► Korean Marines 'chow down' on a meal of American field rations and locally acquired produce. They wear a mixture of Korean and American M56 individual equipment; the centre man has a poncho and M62 canteens on his cartridge belt. (ROKMC)

On return, this process would be reversed so that the individual would arrive back in the States in a service uniform. On Okinawa, piles of rather soiled jungle utilities and boots were left in heaps outside the prefabricated huts used for processing personnel back to the United States. Individuals tended to keep the utility cap, belt, and boots, which were worn at their next duty station to proclaim their status as returning warriors. Since these items were usually unsightly, this lasted until some officer or non-commissioned officer ran the Marine down and told him to send it home. If the individual stayed in the Corps, these items were worn out or thrown away. At the time there was not much sentiment attached to clothing and equipment, with the exception of the above items and possibly the K-Bar knife. Customs and Military Police discouraged efforts to bring anything else home, or even to mail articles back. Photographs and captured enemy items were the exception, and had value as souvenirs. Officers seemed to keep maps and notebooks as well.

An individual was required to mark his personal uniform items with his name at designated locations, generally with a rubber stamp in black block letters over the left shirt pocket and inside the waistband of the trousers. With regards to graffiti numbers and letters on helmets and flak jackets, these could mean a number of things, some fairly obscure. These could include the nine-digit social security number, the older seven-digit service number, or the four-digit military occupational speciality (MOS) number — 0311 for infantryman, 0321 for machine-gunner, 0352 for antitank man, etc. The markings served the practical purpose of identifying individual equipment, even though this was not sanctioned. A Marine's last initial and last four numbers of his social security number could be used to identify his web gear — for example, 'M-4508' — a usefully opaque method when the use of a name would be frowned upon for personalizing government property. Graffiti

also became a means of expressing identity or opinion: names of home states, cities, girlfriends, and nicknames all made this the ground-pounder's equivalent of aircraft nose art. It was a frowned-upon practice in the rear areas, and the bane of the junior officer and non-commissioned officer to control.

Individual or 'tribal' markings were seen in beards, bracelets, necklaces, helmet graffiti, tattoos, even flags. Despite regulation, variety could flourish concurrently within the same theatre of operations depending on the supervision exercised. The longer a unit was in the field the 'grungier' they would look, as uniforms and equipment took on the faded hue of the dust in the local area. Personnel displayed a characteristic 'farmer's' tan on faces, necks, and arms after a few days' exposure to the direct sun. On the subject of grooming, there could be a variation depending on where a person was and how close to a barber shop. Uniform regulations required a haircut to start at the normal hairline from zero to no more than three inches on top. For practical purposes, US

This lieutenant catches up on world events while eating the standard field ration, a 'Meal, Combat, Individual'. He and his men are using their ponchos as improvised lean-tos or 'hooches'. The pristine condition of his uniform indicates an extra set was carried, or more likely, a replacement has recently been received for his old set. Note punctured ration can 'stove' at his feet. (USMC)

Marines did not have sideburns or long hair down the back of the neck (the Vietnamese were not as constrained, but were not given to eccentricities either). Moustaches were allowed, but no beards. At times, lack of water did not allow shaving and 'field' beards resulted. After a while in the bush attitudes and mannerisms differed from the civilized norms of the rear echelon, becoming a source of contention.

While combat operations have been described as a large portion of boring routine with moments of sheer terror or exhilarating pay-back, living conditions when out of action could range from a canvas cot in a squad tent with 12 others, or a canvas and wood South-East Asia hut, to trailers for general officers, and Saigon hotel rooms for some. Even shipboard living for the Marines with the amphibious Special Landing Force was an improvement, as they were dry and well fed by the US Navy.

Rations

Food brings up the whole subject of eating in the field, an item of major concern to most Marines. Meals served at base area mess halls or brought forward to units in 'vat cans' were known as 'A' and 'B' rations. Though issued, mess kits with knife, fork, and spoons were seldom carried or used in the field. This was out of preference and practicality. Water was delivered in green metal or black plastic jerrycans to static positions, or obtained from local sources and

purified with issue Halazone tablets, and carried in canteens. Availability of water was as important as ammunition and medical evacuation on the list of a unit commander's priorities.

Heating meals became a routine task. There was an issue squad stove that was found at the company or battalion command post because of its size, weight, and fuel requirement. Marines on foot made do with heat tabs, a solid Trioxine bar the size of a small candy bar in a dun-coloured foil wrapper. It provided enough heat to boil a single cup of water or warm a single ration can. Heat tabs produced noxious fumes, and were not always even available. A pinch of C4 explosive was also handy and practical, but could be a problem if all demolitions stores in a unit were used up this way. Another heat and light source was to mix liquid bug repellant with the issue ration peanut butter and light it. In most instances rations were eaten cold, as the Marines had neither the time nor the interest for extensive preparation. Another theory was that if you mixed cold and hot meals you would suffer constipation or diarrhoea.

Meals, Combat, Individual or 'C-Rats' were issued in the field. Rations were issued 12 to a box, at the rate of three meals a day. This also included a supply of can openers, the P38 or 'John Wayne' which came with a hole that allowed it to be worn on the dog tag chain or the helmet band. A Marine going on a four-day operation could be issued a whole case (25 lb

◄ Routine operations also had moments of high anxiety, as for these 'Blue Dragon' ROK Marines entering an insurgent-defended hamlet. They are armed with M1 rifles, the man on the right also carries an M79 grenade launcher slung across his back. Below the launcher is a triple-cup bandoleer of the type used to carry 40mm ammunition. All are wearing the distinctive spotted camouflage of the Korean forces. (ROKMC)

weight). He would open all the boxes and discard those items he did not like or could not trade, and pack the rest where he could in his pack or belt kit. This could ensure a weight gain from a steady diet of three meals a day of about 3,300 calories. But because of the terrain and weather, fruit, crackers, and one main or heavy meal a day was about all most would eat, more like 1,100 calories a day, with the end result of a weight loss.

The other means of issue was by unit in the field; this involved a case being issued from battalion to company to platoon to squad. At this level a unit non-commissioned officer (the company gunnery sergeant, the platoon guide, or squad leader) would up-end a case so that the contents were hidden, and issue meals at random to avoid arguments. An experienced small unit leader would mix up the order of the meals in the case, as after a while a Marine knew what meal was located in the case by position. Trash, in turn, was repacked in the meal box and packed in the case to be returned or left.

A meal consisted of the box (to be used as kindling, as a trash holder, or even as a postcard using the printed lid and duty 'free' mail designation. In it were a white plastic spoon (retained for later use, in a helmet band or pocket), an accessory pack, a 'B' unit (crackers, candy, cheese), and the main meal (or heavy). Cigarettes came in the rations in packs of four; these were useful for trading purposes. Coffee

▲ *Others faced the regulars of the North Vietnamese army. These men of the 9th Marines are under fire from 122mm and 130mm artillery firing from the DMZ at outposts set up along the northern border of the Republic of Vietnam. This was one of the reasons for the use of helmets and body armour, despite their weight and bulk. (USMC)*

▶ *In order to cover the approaches to strategic locations from North Vietnam and Laos, the III Marine Amphibious Force built up various helicopter-supplied fire support bases inland to dominate local features and to serve as an anchor for small unit manoeuvres. This hilltop position surrounds a battery of 12th Marine M101 105mm howitzers, the standard Marine field piece in South Vietnam. The defensive positions and living conditions were rudimentary. (USMC)*

was also popular for an early morning or late evening drink.

Preparing a meal was a ritual in itself, consisting of selecting what was to be consumed, preparing a stove from a 'B' unit can, a cup from a fruit can, and consuming it all in the most efficient order: i.e., opening your 'B' unit and putting its contents aside, making the stove, heating your main meal on it at the same time as eating your fruit, so that you had a can to heat your coffee water in while you ate your main meal. Efforts to improve the contents of the main meal involved the use of hot sauce, Worcestershire sauce, and even hot peppers or wild onions. Experience was required to keep from burning yourself and the bottom of your meal, or from having your heat tab burn out before everything was prepared. This was also a way to pass time. . . .

Field rations were used as a medium of exchange with the Vietnamese, for anything from soft drinks to sex. The 'locals' would follow units to beg or salvage left-over rations. Cans were supposed to be crushed to prevent their use as grenades or booby traps (the M26 grenade with its spoon in place would fit inside a ration tin, and when attached to a trip wire it was a deadly device). At times left-over meals were thrown in unit camp fires to be burned, resulting in explosions that sounded like incoming small arms fire: again, a rough way to pass time and to escape boredom.

Brothers in Arms

The Vietnamese Marines remained committed to the defence of the DMZ throughout 1974. First ordered to protect Hue and Da Nang from the Communist attack in spring 1975, the Marines were hastily withdrawn with the collapse of the South Vietnamese in the northern provinces. Five battalion commanders and some 40 company commanders were killed during the fighting. The division reorganized and deployed with its remaining forces at Long Binh in the final battle for Saigon. There it stayed through the subsequent fighting at the end of April 1975. At that point, the Vietnamese Marine Corps ceased to exist except in money and history.

Upon returning to Korea, the ROKMC 2nd Brigade was deployed on its own country's de-militarized zone to maintain the enviable reputation earned in Vietnam as Korea's 'Blue Dragons'. The US Marines resumed almost the same global commitments that they had shouldered before the war, with an emphasis on intervention in times of crisis to protect American lives and property. The collapse of Cambodia and South Vietnam in spring 1975 saw a brief return of air and ground evacuation forces to

▶ Long range artillery support was provided by M107 175mm self-propelled guns. Gunners from the 1st Field Artillery Group serving this piece wear a mix of sateen, jungle, and camouflage utilities. Individual combat equipment was not worn as it hindered movement. The section chief on the left relays firing commands from the battery's executive officer. (USMC)

▶ The job of closing with the enemy still fell to the infantry. These 4th Marine 'grunts' board a Marine Aircraft Group 16 CH-46 at Vandergrift Combat Base to hit North Vietnamese army units in Quang Tri Province in 1969. The men in the foreground wear the OG jungle utility coat over camouflage trousers, M1 helmets, M55 armour vests, and carry PRC25 radios, subsistence loads, and M17 gas masks. The left Marine's M16 is rigged with a 'jungle sling' to carry the weapon in a ready position. (USMC)

◀ *Direct support came from M48 main battle tanks, like this USMC 1st Tank Bn. vehicle with the 5th Marines south-west of Da Nang. The Marine in the foreground displays the carrying limitations of the M41 haversack. (USMC)*

▼ *Close fire came from a commander's 'hip pocket artillery', the M29 81mm mortar of the infantry battalions. These mortarmen of the 4th Marines fire away at the cyclic rate. The weapons pit displays an interesting assortment of gear. Hearing protection and both M52 and M55 armour vest are worn. (USMC)*

withdraw diplomatic personnel and refugees. The experience of Vietnam would remain deeply felt throughout the next two decades, becoming vivid once more among the senior officers and non-commissioned officers who served in the Persian Gulf in 1990–91.

For the Vietnamese, 1975 brought the end of a 30-year civil war in which the Vietnamese Marine Corps played a part until the bitter end. For American and Korean Marines, the Vietnam experience provided new traditions, reputations, and leaders for their respective corps for the next quarter of a century. The weapons, equipment, and even the uniforms have changed; but the spirit remains, forewarning another generation that the price of an élite reputation is paid for in blood.

The problem of the soldier's load continues.

Further reading

Tom Bartlett, editor: *Ambassadors in Green* (Washington, D.C.: Leatherneck Association, 1971)

History and Museums Division: *The Marines in Vietnam, 1954–1973* (Washington, D.C.: Headquarters, US Marine Corps, 1985)

Lt.Gen. Stanley R. Larsen and B.Gen. James L. Collins, Jr.: *Allied Participation in Vietnam* (Washington, D.C.: Department of the Army, 1975)

THE PLATES
(Note: 'right' and 'left' refer to the wearer's right and left, not 'as viewed'.)

A1: USMC general officer, 1969
General Leonard F. Chapman, Jr., Commandant of the US Marines, is depicted wearing the tropical summer service uniform in style during the war. His rank insignia is displayed on his cap and collar; he is wearing the medal ribbons for his personal awards only. This was not a common uniform for wear in Vietnam except in the rear areas.

A2: ROKMC general officer, 1965
Brigadier-General Lee Bong Chool, commander of the ROKMC 2nd Brigade when it arrived in Vietnam. He wears an olive green M56 herringbone twill utility uniform identical to that of the US Marines, distinguished by its hidden buttons on the shirt front and chest pockets. It was common to see both Korean and American uniform items in service.

A3: VNMC general officer, 1970
Lieutenant-General Le Nguyen Khang, Commandant of the Vietnamese Marine Corps and its tactical commander through most of the war, is seen wearing

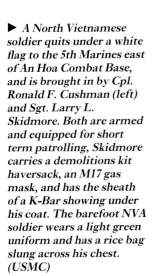

▶ *A North Vietnamese soldier quits under a white flag to the 5th Marines east of An Hoa Combat Base, and is brought in by Cpl. Ronald F. Cushman (left) and Sgt. Larry L. Skidmore. Both are armed and equipped for short term patrolling, Skidmore carries a demolitions kit haversack, an M17 gas mask, and has the sheath of a K-Bar showing under his coat. The barefoot NVA soldier wears a light green uniform and has a rice bag slung across his chest. (USMC)*

The backbone of small unit tactics came from the effective use of M60 medium machine gun teams. This gunner and assistant gunner from the 5th Marines open up during an engagement with an enemy force of 50 soldiers south-west of Da Nang. The 'A' gunner's responsibility was to spot for the machine gunner, who seldom had a clear view of a target from behind the gun. Both wear M1 helmets, M55 armour vests, and M41 haversacks over T-shirts. (USMC)

the distinct Vietnamese 'sea-wave' camouflage uniform without service or unit insignia. He is wearing a black belt and brass buckle similar to that of US Marine advisors.

B1: VNMC infantry combat uniform, 1965

The standard ARVN olive green uniform was worn for initial training and fatigue duties by Marines. This sergeant wears a full size rank insignia on the shirt front instead of the shoulder straps. The beret was navy blue with the brass Marine Infantry badge prior to the adoption of the green beret. The combat equipment is a mixture of American designed web gear.

B2: VNMC service insignia

When the Vietnamese Marine Corps became a distinct service, it adopted an insignia for wear on the right breast pocket of the field uniform. The emblem, used to promote service rather than individual unit identity, was woven or printed in the colours shown. The inscription reads 'Honour and Country'.

B3: VNMC Officer, combat uniform, 1965

The characteristic 'sea-wave' camouflage uniform adopted by the Vietnamese Marines was worn without emblems other than rank insignia and the beret with badge through 1965. This second lieutenant is part of an honour guard. He wears a green beret with gold woven badge, black and silver rank insignia, and a scarf in blue for the VNMC 1st Infantry Battalion. Other insignia were added subsequently.

C1: VNMC service dress, 1965

Seasonal uniforms were available, including khaki dress with service cap as worn by this student at the Marine Corps Schools at Quantico, Virginia. The winter uniform consisted of a dark brown blouse with shoulder board rank insignia, white shirt, black tie, and brown trousers.

C2: VNMC squad leader; Delta region, 1967

This small unit leader wears the camouflage uniform with field equipment in the Mekong River Delta. Visible on his right breast is the service emblem, on his left shoulder the Marine Brigade unit emblem. He carries an American-made Thompson .45 calibre sub-machine gun, and offensive and smoke grenades on his M56 personal equipment. He wears canvas and rubber 'Bata' boots.

C3: VNMC artillery officer, Saigon, 1968

Officer uniforms were identical to the enlisted uniform, but were subject to better tailoring and details. This forward observer is calling in an artillery fire mission in Saigon during the Tet Offensive. He has a pistol in a shoulder holster, but is really armed with his map and radio. The brigade patch is worn on his left shoulder, and over his right pocket is a name tape in the artillery battalion colours of red letters on a white background. No service emblem is worn.

D1: VNMC parade dress, 1969

The camouflage combat uniform was so associated with the Vietnamese Marines that it was used in lieu of a dress uniform during the war. This was achieved for public occasions by adding medals or ribbons, unit award fourragères, coloured neck scarves, parade aiguillettes, white gloves and belts.

D2: VNMC grenadier; Quang Tri City, 1972

At times, supply availability caused variations in the issue of clothing. In this case a Marine is wearing the ARVN Airborne camouflage pattern without service or unit insignia. His weapon is the M79 grenade launcher, and his condition reflects the bitter fighting to recapture the Quang Tri Citadel. His combat equipment is the American M56 pattern.

D3: VNMC advisor; Hue City, 1973

American Marines served with the Vietnamese Marines up to the ceasefire in 1973. They were part of the naval advisory group, and wore VNMC uniforms with the addition of a black-on-green 'U.S. Marines' name tape over the left pocket. Both American and Vietnamese rank insignia were worn to avoid confusion. Depicted is the last senior Marine advisor, Colonel Joshua Dorsey.

E1: ROKMC enlisted utility uniform, 1965

When the Koreans arrived in South Vietnam, they wore their own version of the American M56 and M58 utility uniforms with M41 individual equipment and World War Two era small arms. In some cases, uniforms and equipment were from American assistance programme stocks complete with US Marine markings.

E2: ROKMC service insignia

This Korean Marine Corps insignia was stamped in black ink on the left breast pocket of the utility uniform with the abbreviation for 'Korean Marines'. Variations existed with characters across the top or bottom of the emblem. Like the Americans, the desire was to promote service rather than unit loyalty.

The price of closing with the enemy was paid in dead and wounded Marines. Hospitalman 3rd Class N.W. Jones, a corpsman with the 7th Marines, treats a casualty during Operation *'Oklahoma Hills' as a medical evacuation request is sent by the radio operator on the left. The individual in the rear has an M17 gas mask hanging off his canteen. (USMC)*

E3: ROKMC rifleman; Tuy Hoa, 1966

Officer field uniforms were the same design as the enlisted with the exception of rank insignia on the collars and on headgear. In some cases these were woven directly onto the uniform. This figure is wearing an M1 helmet and cover, M52 body armour, and is armed with an M1 carbine.

F1: ROKMC infantry officer; Tra Binh, 1967

The Koreans made a camouflage utility uniform in their own distinctive five-colour pattern. It had the same construction as the M58 utility uniform, but later versions were simpler, with open patch pockets. The full range of insignia was not used in all instances with this uniform as it became standard issue for use in Vietnam. This figure is based on an early brigade hero, Major Lee In Ho, who was killed in a grenade duel inside an underground enemy position. He is armed with an M1 carbine and wears the M55 body armour and the M1 helmet with American cover.

F2: ROKMC insignia placement

Korean rank placement consisted of collar emblems for officers, and enlisted insignia worn on the left breast pocket. Sleeve grade insignia existed for service and field uniforms, but did not appear to be used in Vietnam. The service insignia was printed on the left pocket over the heart. Over the right breast pocket was a woven name and number tag in gold characters on red.

F3: ROKMC rifleman; Hoi An, 1970

The Korean Marines were noted for a high standard of dress, but even they modified this, as the war progressed, for reasons of comfort and simplicity. In this example, a rifleman is dressed in the camouflage uniform without insignia. His trousers hang loose over full leather boots. His M55 body armour has been modified to carry magazines across the back. He wears a mix of M56 and M61 equipment. A field dressing is fastened to his bayonet scabbard for ease of access.

G1: USMC rifleman; Chu Lai, 1965

American Marines arrived in Vietnam with a temperate climate uniform that had been in use since the late 1950s. His M1 helmet has a green-side cloth cover for camouflage. This Marine is armed with the M14 rifle. He wears a mix of M41 and M61 combat equipment, to include the M61 magazine pouches, a double-pocket grenade pouch, M10 aluminium canteens and covers, a jungle first aid kit, and an M6 bayonet on his right side. He wears his trousers loose over full leather boots.

G2: USMC service insignia

The US Marine 'eagle, globe, and anchor' was worn on the left breast pocket. This insignia was stencilled, embroidered, or applied from a heat transfer. When

During 1970–71 the withdrawal of allied forces and the return of the war to the Vietnamese was well underway. The tempo of operations for the South Vietnamese increased with cross-border operations into Cambodia and Laos. For the remaining allied Marines, security tasks continued. This Korean Marine 'rides shotgun' in the back of a truck in a convoy from Hoi An to Da Nang. His M1 helmet has a bandoleer strap to hold leaves in place; he wears a M55 armour vest, modified Korean camouflage utilities, and leather boots. His uniform displays a characteristic lack of markings. (USMC)

unit issue of clothing occurred the insignia had to be added, or was not worn at all. This form of marking had been standard on Marine field uniforms since World War Two.

G3: USMC helicopter pilot; Da Nang, 1965

Marine flight crews wore a cotton khaki one-piece coverall, standard naval aviation equipment rather than uniform issue. A rectangular leather embossed nametag was worn on the left breast bearing the name, rank, and aviation wings. Various types of headgear were worn when not flying, including baseball caps and utility covers. This pilot wears his .38 calibre revolver survival weapon in a shoulder holster.

H1: USMC radio operator; Da Nang, 1966

As Marines began active combat, the field uniform was modified to the local conditions for comfort and utility. This radioman has cut off the sleeves of his shirt; he either wears no undershirt or has one locally dyed a green colour. The M55 body armour became a routine item of wear. He carries a PRC10 field radio and wears a mix of M41 and M61 equipment for his M14 rifle.

H2: USMC combat engineer; Phu Bai, 1966

Early on, specialized clothing was made available, including uniforms and boots. This engineer wears the first pattern jungle utility trousers and cloth and leather jungle boots. He is engaged in a road sweep for land mines with an electronic 'mine sweeper', and is not carrying any more gear than is needed for this task. He wears an M1 helmet, an M55 armoured vest over the issue white undershirt, and a pistol belt holding a .45 pistol, magazine pouch, and first aid dressing. The power pack for the detector is carried in the leg pocket of his trousers. Armoured shorts and boots were issued, but seldom worn, as they hindered movement.

H3: USMC ANGLICO team member; Marble Mountain, 1967

By this date lightweight jungle utilities were common, even in support units. They were cooler and dried quicker than the standard utilities. One of the three jump-qualified units in Vietnam were the supporting arms co-ordination teams of the air-naval-

The withdrawal of major US Marine combat forces began in 1969 and was completed by June 1971 when the 3rd Marine Amphibious Brigade left Da Nang. These members of the 9th Marines parade their colours on returning to Okinawa, where the 3rd Marine Division assumed duties as part of the Pacific Commands force in readiness. They wear camouflage uniforms for the occasion, complete with 'dog tags' in their jungle boots. The organizational colours were scarlet and gold, with battle streamers suspended from the peak of the staff. (USMC)

ground-liaison company (ANGLICO). This man prepares to conduct a 'pay and proficiency' jump wearing a standard MC1 personnel parachute and T10 reserve. He carries minimal combat equipment, including the K-Bar knife, M41 haversack, and an M3 sub-machine gun.

I1: USMC mortarman; De-Militarized Zone, 1967

Marine infantrymen along the DMZ carried everything needed to fight and survive because of terrain and weather and, in part, because they lacked the luxury of constant helicopter support enjoyed by US Army units. This saw some back-breaking transport loads going into operations, as shown on this mortarman. This epitomizes the origin of the term 'grunt' for the war's combat infantryman. He is using an M43 packboard to carry his M41 haversack, M43 entrenching tool, M62 canteen and cover, and M56 ammunition pouches for his M14 rifle. His canned

The Korean Marines left between December 1971 and January 1972. The commander of ROK Forces Vietnam attaches a unit citation to ROKMC 2nd Bde. colours at Hoi An prior to their departure. The brigade commander, Brig.Gen. Lee Dong Ho, is on the right in camouflage uniform. The Korean Marine colours were scarlet and gold. (USMC)

The Vietnamese Marine Corps was left to fight on, but now at division strength, and considered to be one of the best formations in the Republic of Vietnam Armed Forces, after its 1972 victories. Operationally, it was tied to the defence of I Corps by the threat of North Vietnamese forces, and still provided a strategic reserve for the Joint General Staff. These Marines are drawn up in parade order at the division base camp at Tu Duc. The dress uniform consisted of the combat uniform, with regulation insignia, and the addition of unit fourragère and a white parade aiguillette. M1 helmets, M16 rifles, and M56 equipment belts are displayed as they present arms. (VNMC)

rations hang in the stocking dangling off the back.

I2: USMC armoured crewman; Hue City, 1968
Armoured vehicles used by the US Marines included M48 main battle tanks, amphibious tractors, and Ontos antitank vehicles. Crews wore clothing similar to the one shown here, including the fibreglass combat vehicle crew (CVC) helmet, M44 goggles, M55 body armour, and .45 calibre pistol in an issue shoulder holster. Sometimes worn in lieu of utilities was this one-piece olive green cotton coverall, which had been around since before World War One for vehicle drivers and mechanics.

I3: USMC artillery officer; Khe Sanh, 1968
In the frontline units the difference between officer and enlisted dress was one of style rather than design. Even this became obscured by location and conditions as leaders and radio operators became special targets for the enemy. Here an artillery forward observer in jungle utilities leaves a forward position on a short term patrol. He is carrying his team's spare radio and is equipped with a rifle rather than a regulation pistol. He has rations and a poncho in the demolition bag slung on his chest to balance the radio. Other characteristic accoutrements would be binoculars, compass, and maps.

J1: USMC rifleman; A Shau Valley, 1969
A rifleman examines a 12.7mm heavy machine gun captured during Operation 'Dewey Canyon' on the border of South Vietnam and Laos. This was a series of large scale encounters with the North Vietnamese army in their base areas late in the war. He is wearing the standard ERDL-pattern camouflage utility uniform of the Marines of III MAF. On his 'utility cover' is the pin-on insignia of a lance corporal; a plastic ration spoon is carried in the pocket of his M55 body armour. His helmet, M16, and web gear lie close at hand.

J2: USMC recon team member, 1970
As the war was turned over to the Vietnamese and large scale American withdrawals occurred, more and more 'economy of force' operations were conducted to keep the enemy off balance. This placed greater demands on the long range patrol units of the Marines, found at both the force and division level.

American Marines returned to Vietnam and South-East Asia as Seventh Fleet ready forces to evacuate American Embassy personnel in 1975. These Marines of the 9th Marine Amphibious Brigade are returning to the USS Okinawa on a CH-53 Sea Stallion after the evacuation of Phnom Penh, Cambodia. They wear sateen utilities and leather boots, M1 helmets, M41 individual equipment, M17 gas masks, and M55 body armour — the standard uniform of the post-Vietnam period. (USMC)

Marine recon patrols relied on stealth, communications, and firepower to hit in the enemies' rear areas. This recon man is dressed and equipped for one of these operations with a cut down 'bush' hat, face paint, ERDL camouflage utilities, and a wide assortment of personal and team equipment. He is armed with an M16 rifle, carries fragmentation and smoke grenades, and has a pair of flight gloves in his hand prior to an insertion.

J3: USMC fixed-wing flight gear; Da Nang, 1970
Flight equipment improved and evolved throughout the war, with specialization based on the type of

aircraft flown. This Marine aviator is preparing to fly a ground support mission late in the war. His one-piece flight suit is made of a flame and flash-retardant Nomex material, as are his leather-faced flight gloves. Extra cloth insignia were absent to prevent burns. His APH6 flying helmet protects his head and eyes. It also positions his oxygen mask and communications equipment. He has a MA2 torso harness that fits his ejection seat, a Z4 anti-blackout ('G') suit, combined with a MK2 life preserver and SV1 survival vest, which carried a .38 calibre revolver and knife.

K1: USMC advisor, MACV-SOG, 1971

Not all Marine advisors served with the Vietnamese Marines. Others worked with South Vietnamese Navy, Army, and special operations units. This gunnery sergeant is assigned to the MACV Special Operations Group maritime studies group based at Da Nang for amphibious reconnaissance and raids along the Vietnamese coast. His uniform is as unconventional as his unit, and consists of a green NVA bush hat, local black shirt and trousers, an NVA web belt, and Chinese magazine pouches for his AK47 assault rifle. His jungle boots and K-Bar are American. He had to resemble the enemy at a distance, but kept an American flag handy for recognition from the air.

K2: USMC helicopter flight gear; Tonkin Gulf, 1972

Helicopter crews wore similar clothing to fixed-wing airmen. The differences were in the use of the SPH3 flying helmet and boom microphone, and the lack of a torso harness and anti-blackout suit. They carried the same life preserver and survival vest. Because of their closer proximity to ground fire, they could also wear M55 armoured vests and special aircrew plate armour. An overseas cap or utility cover was worn when not in flight.

K3: USMC Embassy Guard; Saigon, 1973

After the January 1973 ceasefire and withdrawal the only Marines to remain in any number in South Vietnam were the security guards with the American Embassy. In varying strength throughout the war, there were less than 100 by this time. This sergeant wears the modified dress blue uniform and white personal equipment used by formal sentries in the Corps. He is armed with a .38 calibre revolver, with other weapons available for a backup. Two of the last Marines to die in the war were from this unit.

L1: Vietnamese Marine Division insignia

This emblem was adopted for wear on the upper left arm of the utility uniform when the Vietnamese Marines increased to divisional size. Similar to the

previous brigade patch, it used a green background and a shield shape similar to that used by the Vietnamese Army divisions. The central emblem is identical to the previous design.

L2: ROKMC 2nd Brigade insignia
The Korean Marines wore only their service insignia as a part of the uniform; this emblem for the brigade was used on signs, plaques, and informal 'bear can' pins in South Vietnam.

L3: US Marine Division and Wing insignia
The American Marines had not worn unit insignia on uniforms since the World War Two 'battle flashes'. Shown are the designs for the two divisions and the air wing that served in South Vietnam. These

The Vietnamese Marine Division ceased to exist in 1975 during the fighting that decided the fate of Vietnam and its people, unaided by former allies. This Marine trudges past a dead Communist soldier on the outskirts of Saigon, armed with donated American and captured Communist weapons. For the Vietnamese Marine Corps the consequences of national collapse were worked out on the ground, with the ferocity of other civil wars. (VNMC)

appeared in various forms on equipment, signs, plaques, and pins. Exception was made for the wear of aviation squadron insignia on flight clothing.

(Note: colour photographs of USMC and VNMC uniforms and insignia, and USMC personal equipment variations, will be found in *Vietnam: US Uniforms in Colour Photographs* by Kevin Lyles; Windrow & Greene Ltd., London 1992; ISBN 1 872004 52 0.)

INDEX

(References to illustrations are shown in **bold**. Plates are shown with page and caption locators in brackets.)